Gangs

Current Issues

ReferencePoint
Press®

San Diego, CA

Select* books in the Compact Research series include:

Current Issues
Animal Experimentation
Conflict in the Middle East
The Death Penalty
DNA Evidence and
    Investigation
Drugs and Sports
Energy Alternatives
Gangs
Genetic Testing
Global Warming and
    Climate Change
Immigration

Islam
National Security
Nuclear Weapons and
    Security
Obesity
Online Social Networking
Stem Cells
Teen Smoking
Terrorist Attacks
Video Games
World Energy Crisis

Diseases and Disorders
ADHD
Anorexia
Bipolar Disorders
Drug Addiction
HPV
Obsessive-Compulsive
    Disorder

Phobias
Post-Traumatic Stress
    Disorder
Self-Injury Disorder
Sexually Transmitted
    Diseases

Drugs
Antidepressants
Club Drugs
Cocaine and Crack
Hallucinogens
Heroin
Inhalants
Marijuana

Methamphetamine
Nicotine and Tobacco
Painkillers
Performance-Enhancing
    Drugs
Prescription Drugs
Steroids

Energy and the Environment
Coal Power
Garbage and Recycling
Nuclear Power

Solar Power
Toxic Waste
Wind Power

*For a complete list of titles please visit www.referencepointpress.com.

Gangs

Peggy J. Parks

Current Issues

ReferencePoint
Press®

San Diego, CA

© 2011 ReferencePoint Press, Inc.

For more information, contact:
ReferencePoint Press, Inc.
PO Box 27779
San Diego, CA 92198
www. ReferencePointPress.com

Picture credits:
Cover: iStockphoto.com
AP Images: 17
Landov: 12
Steve Zmina: 33–35, 47–48, 60–62, 74–75

LIBRARY OF CONGRESS CATALOGING-IN-PUBLICATION DATA

Parks, Peggy J., 1951–
  Gangs / by Peggy J. Parks.
    p. cm. -- (Compact research series)
  Includes bibliographical references and index.
  ISBN-13: 978-1-60152-114-9 (hardback)
  ISBN-10: 1-60152-114-6 (hardback)
  1. Gangs—United States—Juvenile literature. 2. Violent crimes—United States—Prevention—Juvenile literature. I. Title.
  HV6439.U5P37   2010
  364.1'0660973—dc22

                                                     2010004235

Contents

Foreword

As modern civilization continues to evolve, its ability to create, store, distribute, and access information expands exponentially. The explosion of information from all media continues to increase at a phenomenal rate. By 2020 some experts predict the worldwide information base will double every 73 days. While access to diverse sources of information and perspectives is paramount to any democratic society, information alone cannot help people gain knowledge and understanding. Information must be organized and presented clearly and succinctly in order to be understood. The challenge in the digital age becomes not the creation of information, but how best to sort, organize, enhance, and present information.

ReferencePoint Press developed the *Compact Research* series with this challenge of the information age in mind. More than any other subject area today, researching current issues can yield vast, diverse, and unqualified information that can be intimidating and overwhelming for even the most advanced and motivated researcher. The *Compact Research* series offers a compact, relevant, intelligent, and conveniently organized collection of information covering a variety of current topics ranging from illegal immigration and deforestation to diseases such as anorexia and meningitis.

The series focuses on three types of information: objective single-author narratives, opinion-based primary source quotations, and facts and statistics. The clearly written objective narratives provide context and reliable background information. Primary source quotes are carefully selected and cited, exposing the reader to differing points of view. And facts and statistics sections aid the reader in evaluating perspectives. Presenting these key types of information creates a richer, more balanced learning experience.

For better understanding and convenience, the series enhances information by organizing it into narrower topics and adding design features that make it easy for a reader to identify desired content. For example, in *Compact Research: Illegal Immigration*, a chapter covering the economic impact of illegal immigration has an objective narrative explaining the various ways the economy is impacted, a balanced section of numerous primary source quotes on the topic, followed by facts and full-color illustrations to encourage evaluation of contrasting perspectives.

The ancient Roman philosopher Lucius Annaeus Seneca wrote, "It is quality rather than quantity that matters." More than just a collection of content, the *Compact Research* series is simply committed to creating, finding, organizing, and presenting the most relevant and appropriate amount of information on a current topic in a user-friendly style that invites, intrigues, and fosters understanding.

Gangs at a Glance

Gangs and Gang Members

The U.S. Department of Justice estimates that more than 20,000 gangs with a total of about 1 million members are criminally active in the United States.

Gang Migration

Gangs are no longer confined to large cities. The FBI states that gang activity is rapidly spreading to outlying suburban and rural communities throughout the United States.

Types of Gangs

Four main types of gangs identified by the U.S. Department of Justice are street gangs, outlaw motorcycle gangs, prison gangs, and military gangs.

Gangs and Crime

Law enforcement officials say that gangs commit a wide range of crimes, including distribution of drugs, weapons trafficking, drive-by shootings, armed robbery, assault, identity theft, and homicide. In many communities gangs are responsible for as much as 80 percent of crime.

Cities with Gang Problems

The U.S. Department of Justice has identified Los Angeles, Chicago, and New York as the top three cities for the most gangs and gang-related crime.

Reasons for Joining Gangs

Young people join gangs for many reasons including the desire to belong to a family-like group, protection from rival gangs, the ability to make money (usually from stealing or selling drugs), prestige, and ready access to drugs.

Quitting Gangs

Whether people are able to leave gangs depends on the particular gang and its rules. Jumping out (being beaten by gang members) is a common way of letting someone out. Some gangs expect their members to remain committed for life and threaten them with death if they try to quit.

Fighting Gang Violence

In cities throughout the United States, the FBI and state and local law enforcement officials are focusing on the most violent street gangs in an effort to capture their leaders and get them off the streets.

Overview

Gangs are morphing, multiplying, and migrating—entrenching themselves not just in our inner cities but increasingly in our ever-sprawling suburbs and wide-open rural spaces.”

—Federal Bureau of Investigation, a law enforcement agency of the U.S. Department of Justice.

“**Gangs and gang-involved kids exist at some level in every community. Certain groups have decided to use violence and retribution, and their acts are affecting all of us.**”

—Steven D. Strachan, the chief of police of Kent, Washington, a suburb of Seattle.

At 16 years old, Melody Ross was thoroughly enjoying life. She had just begun her junior year at Wilson High School in Long Beach, California, where she was an honors student and a pole-vaulter on the track team. She was popular and known for being friendly, kind, and someone who always had a sunny smile on her face. On the evening of October 30, 2009, Melody and her friends went to their school's homecoming football game. After the game ended, the girls left the stadium and were sitting on the curb in front of the school. Suddenly the loud crack of gunshots filled the air. A feud had broken out between members of rival gangs, and they were shooting at each other—with bystanders caught in the crossfire.

By the time the violence ended, three people lay on the ground, wounded and bleeding: two men and Melody. Ambulances rushed them

10

to the hospital, where the men were treated for non-life-threatening injuries. Melody, however, was not so fortunate. She died of a severe bullet wound in her side. Her family and friends were devastated, and as a memorial to her, a classmate named Dylan Vassberg created a Facebook page entitled *RIP Melody Ross*. "Every kid our age—we don't ever think we're going to die," he says. "We never think that. We think we're going to college and we're going to have a long life and die of old age. Not die because someone decided to shoot a gun. We never think of that. It's not something that crosses our mind ever. Not even fathomable, really."[1]

How Serious a Problem Are Gangs?

Although the precise number of gangs and gang members (known as gangbangers) is not known, the U.S. Department of Justice makes estimates based on information it receives from state and local law enforcement officials. In January 2009 the Justice Department's National Gang Intelligence Center released a report entitled *National Gang Threat Assessment 2009*. The report states that more than 20,000 violent gangs with a total of approximately 1 million members were criminally active in the United States as of September 2008.

The report's authors state that "gangs pose a serious threat to public safety." They warn that throughout the country, gang activity is rapidly spreading from large cities to outlying suburban and rural areas. This, they predict, will cause gang-related violent crime to remain at high levels and likely increase. They write: "As these gangs encounter resistance from local gangs or other drug distributors in these communities, an increase in violent incidents such as assaults, drive-by shootings, and homicides can be expected."[2]

The Evolution of Gangs

No one knows exactly when gangs first formed, but they are often assumed to have been around for centuries. According to Lou Savelli, who is a retired New York City police sergeant and cofounder of the East Coast Gang Investigators Association, the word *thug* dates back to India during the 1200s. It is derived from "Thugz," an Indian word that referred to a gang of criminals who traveled throughout the country terrorizing towns. Savelli adds that like gangs today, the Thugz had their own symbols, hand signs, slang language, and rituals.

Members of the Eastside Crips flash gang signs at the Los Angeles funeral of one of the founders of their gang. The Justice Department estimates that more than 20,000 gangs are involved in criminal activities in the United States—and not just in big cities.

Gang activity is thought to have begun in the United States early in the country's history. Journalist Ed Grabianowski explains: "Criminal gangs have certainly been around as long as crime itself—it doesn't take a criminal mastermind to realize there is strength in numbers. The urbanization that accompanied the Industrial Revolution gave rise to the modern street gang."[3] Throughout the 1800s, as more people immigrated to America from other countries, gangs such as the Monk Eastman Gang and Five Points Gang formed and terrorized the streets of New York. But it was the 1920s that ushered in the heyday of gang activity in the

United States because of a notorious gangster named Al Capone, also called Scarface.

This was a time known as Prohibition, when the Eighteenth Amendment to the Constitution made the sale or distribution of alcohol illegal. Supporters hoped the legislation would transform American society for the better, but its effects were quite different from what they expected. Once alcohol was no longer legally available, criminal gangs began to distribute it on the black market. These gangs developed rapidly and continued to grow in power, which caused a steep rise in violent crime. Capone and his gang of criminals were responsible for a wave of violence in the Chicago area during the 1920s and 1930s. Savelli says this led to his becoming known as most violent gangster in Chicago and perhaps in all of the United States. Capone's reputation spread far and wide, and his actions strongly influenced the activities of would-be gangsters throughout the country. By the time Prohibition ended in 1933, gangs had become entrenched throughout the country and were widely known for their connections with violent crime.

During the 1950s gang-related crime was rampant in a number of U.S. cities, including Los Angeles, Chicago, and New York, and it was steadily growing. Over the following decades gangs became better organized and continued to expand their activities from cities into neighboring communities, as the Justice Department explains: "The gang members who migrated from urban areas often formed new, neighborhood-based local gangs. These local gangs generally controlled their territories through violence and intimidation."[4] Gang membership—and associated violent crime—continued to grow throughout the rest of the twentieth century and into the twenty-first.

> " **Gangs often differ significantly from one another based on membership requirements, structure, and the ages and ethnicity of the members.** "

Street Gangs and Motorcycle Outlaws

Gangs often differ significantly from one another based on membership requirements, structure, and the ages and ethnicity of the members.

Two main types that have been identified by law enforcement officials are street gangs and outlaw motorcycle gangs. The Justice Department says that street gangs pose a considerable threat to communities because they are the largest group and also control the greatest geographical area. "Therefore," Justice Department authorities explain,

> criminal activities such as violence and drug trafficking perpetrated by street gangs pose the greatest threat. The threat becomes magnified as national- and regional-level street gangs migrate from urban areas to suburban and rural communities, expanding their influence in most regions and broadening their presence outside the United States to develop associations with . . . criminal organizations in Mexico, Central America, and Canada.[5]

Most street gangs are local-level gangs that operate in single locations while regional-level street gangs are more organized and larger. Some of the largest and most violent street gangs are Hispanic gangs such as MS-13, 18th Street, Sureños, and Almighty Latin King and Queen Nation (Latin Kings) and the predominately African American gangs Bloods, Crips, and Black P. Stone Nation. Asian gangs such as the Asian Boyz are also developing a reputation as a result of their links to drug trafficking and violent crimes. Though less common than gangs of other racial and ethnic groups, white gangs also pose a threat. The white supremacist street gang Nazi Lowriders has a growing presence in Southern California, Arizona, Colorado, Florida, and Illinois, and members have been connected with a number of racially motivated violent crimes.

> **As of September 2008, more than 147,000 documented gang members were incarcerated in federal, state, and local correctional facilities.**

Outlaw motorcycle gangs also pose a significant threat because they engage in numerous criminal activities, such as trafficking in weapons and drugs, and often commit violent crimes. State and local law enforcement agencies have identified as many as 520 outlaw motorcycle gangs with an estimated total of 20,000 members of various races and ethnicities. The motorcycle gangs that the FBI considers the greatest threat because of criminal activities are the Sons of Silence, Bandidos, Mongols, Hells Angels, and Outlaws.

Gangs Behind Bars

Just because people are incarcerated, and even sentenced to life in prison, does not necessarily prevent them from engaging in gang activities. According to the Justice Department, prison gangs are highly structured criminal networks that are active within prisons throughout the United States. It adds that as of September 2008, more than 147,000 documented gang members were incarcerated in federal, state, and local correctional facilities. One state where this is a particularly serious problem is Washington. According to a study released in 2009, gang-affiliated inmates are responsible for 43 percent of all violent crimes that are committed in the state's prisons. The report also states that the Crips are the most represented prison gang, with 2,385 inmate members. Also well known for violence behind bars is the white supremacist gang Aryan Brotherhood and the Latino gangs Barrio Azteca and Mexican Mafia.

> "Although gangs have a presence in communities all over the United States, the National Gang Center says that the three cities with the most gangs and worst gang-related crime are Los Angeles, Chicago, and New York."

One gang that has been especially violent in Texas prisons is the Texas Syndicate. In February 2007 federal authorities issued indictments for gang members who were suspected of being responsible for as many as 16 murders outside the state's prisons, including a triple slaying in 2003. The indictment states: "It is understood that members and prospects of the TS may receive a telephone call and instructions to commit a murder . . . at any time. Regardless of the member's friendship or association with the victim, the orders are to be carried out."[6]

Not only are gangs extremely active in prisons, gang members who have been imprisoned are often the gangs' top leaders. According to

Sergeant Jeremy Young, who is a supervisor with the Modesto, California, police street crimes unit, the bottom level of a gang's chain of command is made up of gangbangers who are the "soldiers" on the street; the mid-level is composed of the leaders of street crews who run the operation; and the top level are the bosses who are often inside prisons. "The (gang leaders in the) prisons run the street," he says. "A lot of things that start in there end up out here."[7]

Criminal Activities

Gangs are involved in a wide range of crimes. These include drug distribution, assault, armed robbery, drive-by shootings, auto theft, identity theft, extortion, weapons trafficking, and homicide. In fact, the *National Gang Threat Assessment* report says that according to law enforcement officials throughout the United States, criminal gangs commit as much as 80 percent of the crime in many communities.

Yet the connection between gangs and crime is a controversial issue. According to the Justice Policy Institute, a Washington, D.C.–based think tank that supports alternatives to incarceration, gang members are not responsible for the biggest share of crime in most jurisdictions. In a July 2007 report, the group states that many crimes committed by gang members are unrelated to gang activity, and reliable data on the extent of gang crime do not exist. The report's authors write: "The available evidence indicates that gang members play a relatively small role in the national crime problem. . . . National estimates and local research findings suggest that gang members may be responsible for fewer than one in 10 homicides; fewer than one in 16 violent offenses; and fewer than one in 20 serious . . . crimes."[8]

Gang-Infested Cities

Although gangs have a presence in communities all over the United States, the National Gang Center says that the three cities with the most gangs and worst gang-related crime are Los Angeles, Chicago, and New York. According to John S. Pistole, who is the deputy director of the FBI, Los Angeles is "ground zero for modern gang activity," with over 400 gangs and an estimated 40,000 gang members. "Many gangs were born here, a generation ago," he says. "But they are no longer limited to Los Angeles. Like a cancer, gangs are spreading to communities across America."[9]

Federal officials discuss the arrests of more than 2,000 illegal immigrants, including many gang members. A poster shows photographs of one arrested illegal immigrant with his gang tattoos. Illegal immigrant gang members are a growing concern for law enforcement.

Two other California cities where gang-related crime is increasing are San Diego, where gang-related homicides rose 56 percent between 2006 and 2007, and Salinas, where gang-related homicides increased 125 percent during that same period of time. Gangs are also a serious problem in Hartford, Connecticut, and Camden, New Jersey. And Pistole adds that gangs are becoming more active in many other cities including Baltimore, Houston, Washington, D.C., Denver, Atlanta, Indianapolis, New Orleans, and Omaha, Nebraska.

High-Tech Gangbanging

The Internet has opened up a whole new way for gangbangers to recruit new members. As a February 2007 ABC News report states: "By posting online content that glorifies the thug lifestyle, gangs are using the Web to recruit—some using children as young as 8 years old as part of the online recruiting process, known as 'Net Banging.'"[10] Sometimes rival gang members spar with each other online, proudly displaying their gang colors, tattoos, and gang hand signs in photos. They also use the Internet to schedule fights with each other as well as brag about crimes that they have committed. By monitoring these sites, federal and state law enforcement officials can track gang activity.

> **Gangbangers communicate with each other by sending text messages, and it is not uncommon for them to use multiple phones that they discard after they have completed criminal operations such as drug trafficking.**

Cell phones also play a crucial role in gang operations. Gangbangers communicate with each other by sending text messages, and it is not uncommon for them to use multiple phones that they discard after they have completed criminal operations such as drug trafficking. The Justice Department offers an example: "The leader of an African American street gang operating on the north side of Milwaukee used more than 20 cell phones to coordinate drug-related activities of the gang: most were prepaid phones that the leader routinely discarded and replaced."[11]

Why Do Young People Join Gangs?

Law enforcement professionals say that the issue of why kids join gangs is complex. According to the Justice Policy Institute, no single risk factor or set of factors can accurately predict which young people will become gang members. One of the most common reasons kids join gangs is that they are from broken homes and desperately want to be part of a family-like group, and they perceive gangs as being able to provide that. Brandon Robinson grew up in a housing project in Kansas City, Missouri. As a participant in a 2007 survey about gangs, he told interviewers that many of those who join share the commonality of being from poverty-stricken, dysfunctional backgrounds. "You got family members on crack and you ain't eating right," he says. "Everybody's hungry."[12]

According to Robinson, gang members look out for each other, help feed each other, and stick up for each other, much like a family would. "That's when you start loving your street,"[13] he says. Other reasons for joining gangs include the lure of having money to spend (from stealing or selling drugs), easy access to drugs, and protection from the dangers of the street and rival gangs. Yet many criminal justice experts say that being part of a gang does not keep kids safer at all. In fact, studies have shown that young people who are involved with gangs have a markedly higher likelihood of being injured or killed than those who are not gang-affiliated.

> " **Many people say that joining a gang is a lifetime commitment, and the only way someone can leave is by dying or going to prison.** "

Girl Gangs

Traditionally, gangs have been dominated by males and that is still true today. But the Justice Department states that female involvement in gangs is on the upswing. A May 2008 study by the Office of Juvenile Justice and Delinquency Prevention found that in high-crime neighborhoods nearly 30 percent of girls surveyed claimed that they were members of gangs. The report ranked "young females as the fastest growing offenders in the national juvenile justice population."[14]

One city that has experienced growing problems with girl gangs is Flint, Michigan. Gina Nyovane, a 22-year-old graduate of Flint Northwestern High School, has observed girl gangs in her former school and throughout the city. She says that these gangs are becoming more widespread and more violent, as she explains: "I hear it all the time. Girls are quick to pull a gun out, faster than a guy."[15] Over Labor Day weekend in 2009, members of a girl gang called the Goonies followed a car that was carrying members of a rival gang, the Dufflebacks. A young man traveling with the Goonies fired six shots at the other car, killing an 18-year-old male passenger and wounding the female driver.

Can People Leave the Gang Life Behind?

The common view is that people who join gangs are never allowed to leave them. The Justice Policy Institute says its research has found that gang membership is not a "one-way street" and that the typical gang member is active for a year or less. The group explains: "This myth is perpetuated not only by the media but also by gang members who exaggerate the stakes of membership in order to underscore the importance and permanence of their collective bond."[16]

Yet many people say that joining a gang is a lifetime commitment, and the only way someone can leave is by dying or going to prison. Former gang member Hashim Garrett was 15 years old when he was shot six times in the back and legs. Today he struggles to walk and must use forearm crutches because his right leg is paralyzed. In a speech to students at a middle school in 2008, Garrett addressed the realities of gang life: "They say they're like your family, but your loved ones don't ask much of you. Come home on time, clean up your room, be polite, eat your vegetables. The gang's going to ask more than that. Hold this gun. Hold these drugs. Prove you're wild. Maybe kill somebody." He adds that most gang members want to quit the gang but are too afraid to do so. "If you join the football team and you don't like the coach, you can quit. You can't quit a gang that easy."[17]

Federal agencies such as the FBI and the Bureau of Alcohol, Tobacco, Firearms, and Explosives have partnered with state and local police departments throughout the United States in an effort to bring down gangs and put an end to their crime sprees.

Can Gang Violence Be Stopped?

Controlling gang proliferation and gang-related crime is one of the most significant challenges facing law enforcement officials every day of the year. Federal agencies such as the FBI and the Bureau of Alcohol, Tobacco, Firearms, and Explosives have partnered with state and local police departments throughout the United States in an effort to bring down gangs and put an end to their crime sprees.

In many cities, the focus is on eliminating the leadership of gang enterprises. According to Pistole, the goal is to do more than just disrupt their activities—it is to "dismantle them entirely." He explains:

> Taking apart a gang is like demolishing a building. Hacking away at individual walls and beams might damage the building, but it doesn't destroy it. But using federal drug and racketeering statutes is akin to dynamiting the foundation. Once the gang's leadership infrastructure implodes, all members are weakened. It becomes difficult for the group to operate. Eventually, it crumbles. And so our strategy is to prosecute as many gang leaders, members, and associates as possible so there are no pieces left which are large enough to allow the gang to rebuild.[18]

How Serious
a Problem
Are Gangs?

❝Following a marked decline from the mid-1990s to the early 2000s, a steady resurgence of gang problems has occurred in recent years.❞

—James C. Howell, Arlen Egley Jr., and Christina O'Donnell, research associates with the National Gang Center.

❝Wherever MS-13 goes, violence follows. Gang members have carried out beheadings and grenade attacks in Central America and have hacked people with machetes in cities along the East Coast in the United States.❞

—Jessica M. Vaughan and John D. Feere, policy analysts with the Center for Immigration Studies.

For people in many areas of the world, including the United States, gang violence is a harsh reality of life. According to the U.S. Department of Justice, the problem in America is growing worse. The Justice Department estimates that the number of gang members totaled about 1 million as of September 2008, which was an increase from 800,000 in 2005. One reason gangs continue to grow larger and more powerful is that they are fostering relationships with criminal organizations in Mexico, Central America, and Canada. This has led to a proliferation of drugs and weapons being smuggled across the U.S. border as well as an influx of illegal aliens who join gangs.

To emphasize the seriousness of America's gang violence, FBI deputy director John Pistole tells the story of a young woman who was working at a Los Angeles outdoor market in September 2007. Her newborn son, Luis, was beside her in his stroller. Members of the 18th Street gang approached one of the market's vendors, telling him that he could not sell his goods in *their* territory unless he paid them rent. He had steadfastly refused to meet their demands in the past, and when he continued to do so at the market, gang members drew their guns and opened fire on him. The man survived, but Luis did not. A stray bullet struck the baby and killed him instantly. Pistole says that this tragic incident is indicative of what is happening throughout the country: "In too many neighborhoods, too many young people are recruited into gangs. They fall into a life of crime, drugs, and violence. They shoot each other, with no regard to the innocent bystanders caught in the crossfire. Crime and violence are not confined to their cliques, but have a chilling effect on entire communities."[19]

A Ruthlessly Vicious Gang

Of all the gangs known to law enforcement, Mara Salvatrucha, or MS-13, is one of the most violent. It started as a small Los Angeles street gang formed during the 1980s by immigrants from El Salvador. Now, however, it is among the largest and most dangerous gangs in the United States and Central America. According to the Bureau of Immigration and Customs Enforcement (ICE), MS-13 has "mushroomed into the size of a small army" and "strives to be the most violent and feared gang in the world."[20] ICE states that MS-13 members have been convicted of murder, assault, extortion, kidnapping, theft, drug dealing, rape, robbery, and other violent crimes.

One city that is plagued by the violence of MS-13 is Houston, Texas. Although larger gangs are active in the city, the FBI considers MS-13 to be "of particular concern because members are often heavily armed and well trained in the use of weapons and assault tactics."[21] In January 2009 MS-13

> " Of all the gangs known to law enforcement, Mara Salvatrucha, or MS-13, is one of the most violent. "

gang members robbed a Houston beauty salon at gunpoint and sexually assaulted an employee. They warned her not to go to the police, saying that if she did she would regret it. They also threatened the salon owner, telling her that they would kill her if she reported the incident, and they demanded that she pay them a weekly protection fee of $100.

The salon owner was terrified—but she was also angry. She had seen the same kinds of crimes committed in her native El Salvador, and she was determined to fight to keep them from happening in her adopted country. Even though she feared for her life and the lives of her family members, she went to the FBI and told agents what happened. During that visit she turned over a security surveillance tape that showed the gang members' faces.

> **Law enforcement officials estimate that 50 to 60 gangs are active in Chicago and that together, they have as many as 30,000 members.**

About a week later the woman had not paid the protection money. In retaliation, two MS-13 gangbangers drove by the salon and sprayed the front door with bullets—but they did not get away with the violent act. Because of the tapes and the salon owner's cooperation, the FBI agents arrested seven members of the gang. As one agent explains: "This case is proof that victims of crime should not suffer in silence." He adds that the salon owner, who was placed in protective custody by the FBI, "was courageous to stand up to gang members, and as a result those gang members are now in jail."[22]

Violent Communities

Located on the shores of Lake Michigan, Chicago is often called one of America's most beautiful cities. With its tree-lined neighborhoods of stately brownstone homes, the "Magnificent Mile" shopping district, prolific theaters and restaurants, and world-renowned museums, the city attracts tourists from many different countries—yet it also has a dark and dangerous side. Law enforcement officials estimate that 50 to 60 gangs are active in Chicago and that together, they have as many as 30,000 members. Armed gangbangers roam the streets of the South Side of Chicago, committing crimes and terrorizing the people who live there. A chilling testament to this gang violence is evident in one of the city's lesser-known monuments: an arrangement of more than 150 landscaping stones, each bearing the name of a school-age child killed by gang violence since 2007. Police superintendent Jody Weis states that Chicago youth have become increasingly more violent over the years. He explains: "There's simply too many gangs, too many guns and too many drugs on the streets. We've got a problem with some of our young people . . . resorting to use of weapons and violence to solve any type of conflicts they may have."[23]

Chicago has had a problem with gang violence for many years, but public outrage was sparked in 2007 when a 16-year-old honors student named Blair Holt was killed. Holt, who was not involved with a gang, was riding in a city bus with a friend when members of rival gangs started shooting at each other. He attempted to shield his friend by pushing her down into a seat. His heroic act saved her life, but he was fatally shot in the stomach. Afterward, his father, a Chicago police officer, expressed his despair and frustration over gangs who do not think twice about killing people: "You wonder where it comes from. What causes a child to wantonly and blatantly hatch such an ill-conceived plan? To go out and do something like this? What makes them do it? Where is this coming from? What are the influences?"[24]

> **Members of every major street gang and some outlaw motorcycle gangs have been identified on both domestic and international military bases.**

Chicago is far from alone in its ongoing struggle with gang violence. It is prevalent in communities all over the country. In South Carolina, for instance, the rate of gang violence has risen nearly 1,000 percent over the past decade, with the highest number of incidents reported in Colleton County. Although Colleton County is home to just 38,000 people, law enforcement investigators have identified about 20 active gangs with an estimated total of 400 members. According to Sheriff George Malone, "The violence in Colleton County is out of control."[25] One incident occurred in November 2009 in the small town of Walterboro. A group of people were playing cards in the front yard of their home when a car pulled up and suddenly opened fire on the group. A 20-month-old toddler and 2 adults were killed; 6 others were injured.

Gangs in the Military

According to the Justice Department, gang activity is on the upswing in the military. Members of every major street gang and some outlaw motorcycle gangs have been identified on both domestic and international military bases. One incident involved three soldiers stationed in Alaska who were charged with murder after killing a civilian as they shot at members of a rival gang. Another involved a soldier who was arrested in October 2007 for the gang-related shooting of five people in Oklahoma. A 2009 *Yale Law Journal* article describes one case in which a marine sergeant who was a gang member "shot his commanding officer and executive officer—both lieutenant colonels—and threatened to continue killing officers until his fellow gang members were released from confinement."[26]

While on active duty, gang members may abuse their security privileges and access to weapons and other military equipment to further gang activities. For instance, military gang members may take advantage of their positions to engage in criminal acts such as trafficking illicit drugs or weapons. According to the same article, a gang member in the army who was stationed in Iraq smuggled home four AK-47 assault rifles that were later used to commit multiple bank robberies.

> **Gang members who are in prison are every bit as threatening as those who are on the streets, especially because gangs who are behind bars often control crimes that are committed outside of prison.**

After gang members have been discharged from the military, they remain a serious threat to society. They can use their combat skills against rival gangs and also teach those skills to others. The Justice Department says that this poses a "potentially significant threat," as it explains: "Gang members with military training pose a unique threat to law enforcement personnel because of the distinctive military skills that they possess . . . especially if gang members trained in weapons, tactics, and planning pass this instruction on to other gang members."[27] The Justice Department adds that such military training could ultimately result in more organized, sophisticated, and dangerous gangs as well as an increase of deadly assaults on law enforcement officers.

Incarcerated Gangs

Incarcerated gang members are every bit as threatening as those who are on the streets because gang members who are behind bars often control crimes that are committed outside of prison. One example is the Mexican Mafia (also known as the Eme), a violent prison gang with as many as 75,000 members. The incarcerated leaders rule over associates who are given the authority to order crimes in neighborhoods or cities. Tony Rafael, the author of the book *The Mexican Mafia*, explains: "Street gangsters very often are puppets of the big homies locked up in prison. The proof is overwhelming and plays itself out on an almost daily basis in almost every neighborhood in Southern California."[28]

Members of the Mexican Mafia and their associates have been connected with kidnapping, murder, drug trafficking, and extortion, among other crimes. According to Rafael, the gang has grown into a large, powerful, and violent organization. He writes: "It has far-reaching intelligence and communications systems, as well as a standing army of thousands of street soldiers."[29] Rafael adds that the Mexican Mafia continues to expand its power over street crime: "Most neighborhoods in Southern California that have a strong Hispanic street gang presence feel the power of the Mexican Mafia. It took local and state law enforcement over twenty years from the founding of the Mexican Mafia to recognize its influence on the streets. It took another two decades for federal law enforcement to address the Eme as a significant criminal organization."[30]

Aside from controlling crime on the streets, these gangs are also involved in violent acts inside prisons. This is a serious problem in Ohio, where attacks in state prisons have doubled from nearly 500 in 2005 to more than 1,000 during 2008. Corrections officials say that part of the increase in violence is due to an influx of gangs such as the Heartless Felons, who are known for attacking prisoners in bands of six or more. Some of the worst violence has broken out at Mansfield Reformatory, a prison built for 1,536 inmates that now houses 2,475—161 percent over capacity. "These are dangerous times," says Shirley Pope, the director of the state's Correctional Institutional Inspection Committee. "Mansfield is overcrowded. It is understaffed and on top of that, it has this peculiar group of younger inmates who have been described as incredibly vicious."[31]

An Ongoing Problem

Whether they are terrorizing people in neighborhoods, committing crimes while in the military, or reigning over street crime from inside prisons, gangs are a significant problem all over the United States. Law enforcement officials report that gangs now have a presence in every U.S. state and the District of Columbia, and gang membership appears to be growing. According to reports from local, state, and federal authorities, there is no sign that this situation will change anytime in the near future.

How Serious a Problem Are Gangs?

66 **Criminal gangs commit as much as 80 percent of the crime in many communities.** 99

—National Gang Intelligence Center and National Drug Intelligence Center, *National Gang Threat Assessment 2009*, January 2009. www.justice.gov.

The National Gang Intelligence Center and National Drug Intelligence Center are agencies of the U.S. Department of Justice.

66 **The available evidence indicates that gang members play a relatively small role in the national crime problem despite their propensity toward criminal activity.** 99

—Judith Greene and Kevin Pranis, *Gang Wars: The Failure of Enforcement Tactics and the Need for Effective Safety Strategies*, Justice Policy Institute, July 2007. www.justicepolicy.org.

Greene and Pranis are criminal justice policy analysts.

Bracketed quotes indicate conflicting positions.

* Editor's Note: While the definition of a primary source can be narrowly or broadly defined, for the purposes of Compact Research, a primary source consists of: 1) results of original research presented by an organization or researcher; 2) eyewitness accounts of events, personal experience, or work experience; 3) first-person editorials offering pundits' opinions; 4) government officials presenting political plans and/or policies; 5) representatives of organizations presenting testimony or policy.

Primary Source Quotes

66 From prison cells in Pelican Bay, members of the Mexican Mafia can order executions on practically any Los Angeles street, throughout most of Southern California, even in neighboring states. 99

—Tony Rafael, *The Mexican Mafia*. New York: Encounter, 2007, p. vii.

Rafael is a writer from Los Angeles who has researched gangs for more than 10 years.

66 Unlike what most people believe, on the East Coast, there is more Blood-on-Blood killings than Blood vs. Crip. 99

—Dashaun Morris, *War of the Bloods in My Veins*. New York: Scribner, 2008, p. 166.

Morris is a former Bloods gang leader who now works with young people who are at risk of joining gangs.

66 Gangs threaten our society, from city streets to suburban neighborhoods and beyond. They bring a culture of violence and drugs to our doorsteps, creating an atmosphere of fear, diminishing the quality of life, and endangering the safety, well-being, and future of our children. 99

—Michael B. Mukasey, *Attorney General's Report to Congress on the Growth of Violent Street Gangs in Suburban Areas*, April 2008. www.justice.gov.

Mukasey is the former attorney general of the United States.

66 Not all gang members are anti-social and violent, and some have shown us that they want to be a positive contributing member of our society. 99

—David Kerr, "Addict Gang Members Helping Each Other," Newark blog, November 4, 2008. www.nj.com.

Kerr runs Integrity House in Newark, New Jersey, which provides substance abuse treatment and support services.

❝Data on gang membership and gang crime are notoriously subjective. . . . A major problem is that abstract terms like 'affiliation' and 'integration' are often used in government and media reporting alike in this context without concrete definition or specific example.❞

—Tom Diaz, "Could Latino Street Gangs Transform Themselves into Transnational Drug Mafias?" Crime Report, June 9, 2009. http://thecrimereport.org.

Diaz is a lawyer and author and a senior policy analyst at the Violence Policy Center.

....

❝Gang violence is an attack not only on individuals, but on our communities. It stops mothers from allowing their children to play outside. It prevents the elderly from taking walks in their neighborhoods. It creates an environment of fear.❞

—Dianne Feinstein, "Priorities: Combating Criminal Street Gangs," Dianne Feinstein Web site, 2009. http://feinstein.senate.gov.

Feinstein is a U.S. senator from California.

....

❝No community should have to live with violent gangs in their midst.❞

—Tracy Siska, "Gangs, Violent Crime, and Unintended Consequences in Chicago," *Huffington Post*, August 15, 2008. www.huffingtonpost.com.

Siska is executive director of the Chicago Justice Project.

....

❝Gangs and gang-involved kids exist at some level in every community. Certain groups have decided to use violence and retribution, and their acts are affecting all of us.❞

—Steven D. Strachan, "Four Myths That Complicate Efforts to Confront Gang Violence," *Seattle Times*, January 29, 2009. http://seattletimes.nwsource.com.

Strachan is chief of police in Kent, Washington.

....

How Serious a Problem Are Gangs?

- The U.S. Department of Justice states that as of September 2008 about **1 million** gang members belonging to more than **20,000** gangs were active in all 50 U.S. states and the District of Columbia.

- Studies have shown that nearly **150,000** gang members are incarcerated in federal, state, and local correctional facilities.

- Based on reporting over a five-year period ending in 2007, **94.3 percent** of gang-related homicides involved the use of a firearm.

- According to the U.S. Department of Justice, as many as **520** outlaw motorcycle gangs are active throughout the United States with more than **20,000** members.

- The Bureau of Immigration and Customs Enforcement (ICE) states that the **MS-13** gang, with roots in El Salvador, is active in 48 U.S. states, Washington, D.C., and Puerto Rico, as well as in Honduras, Guatemala, and parts of Mexico and Canada.

- In 2008, **58 percent** of state and local law enforcement officials reported that criminal gangs were active in their jurisdictions, compared with **45 percent** in 2004.

- The U.S. Department of Justice states that **neighborhood-based street gangs** account for the largest number of gangs in the United States.

Gang Activity by U.S. Region

According to the U.S. Department of Justice, gangs are active in many parts of the United States. The highest amount of gang activity is in the Pacific region followed by the Southeast, which saw a steady increase in gang activity between 2004 and 2008.

Percent of State and Local Law Enforcement Agencies Reporting Gang Activity

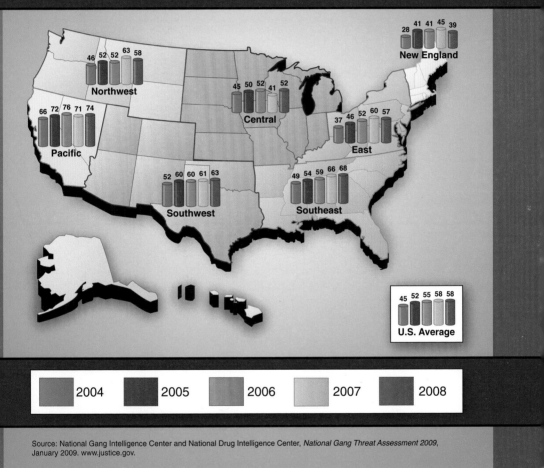

| | 2004 | 2005 | 2006 | 2007 | 2008 |

Source: National Gang Intelligence Center and National Drug Intelligence Center, *National Gang Threat Assessment 2009*, January 2009. www.justice.gov.

- According to the Web site Street Gangs.com, an estimated **137 Asian** gangs are active throughout Los Angeles County.

- The U.S. Department of Justice states that criminal gangs commit as much as **80 percent** of crimes in many communities.

Bloods Are the Most Prominent Gang in America

The U.S. Department of Justice states that as of September 2008 approximately 1 million gang members belonging to more than 20,000 gangs were involved in criminal activities in the United States. According to reports by attendees at the 2007 World Gang Control Strategy Summit, the Bloods (a predominantly African American gang) represent the most prominent gang, with hybrid gangs (small gangs that have banded together) and Hispanic gangs the fastest growing. This graph shows the breakdown of some of the country's largest gangs.

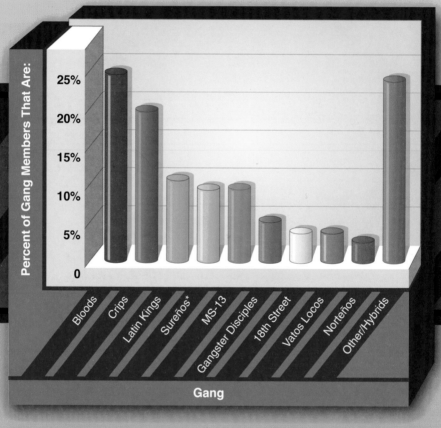

*Sureño gangs have been identified as individual gangs and also local gangs and their affiliation to Sureño gangs, such as Vatos Locos (Sur 13).

Source: National Alliance of Gang Investigators' Associations, *2007 World Gang Control Strategy Summit Report*, August 2008. www.cgiaonline.org.

- According to an April 2008 report from the U.S. Department of Justice, approximately **80 percent** of 18th Street gang members in California are illegal aliens from Mexico and Central America.

South Carolina's Battle with Gangs

Between 1998 and 2007 gang-related crimes steadily rose in South Carolina, from 105 incidents to 1,304 incidents—an increase of more than 1,000 percent. This graph shows the growth of gang violence over the 10-year period.

Gang-Related Crime in South Carolina – 1998 to 2007

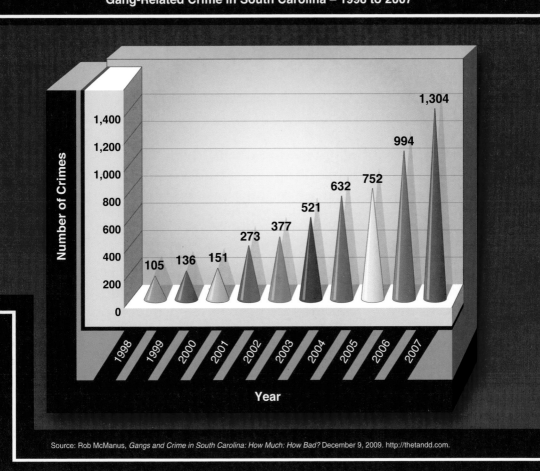

Source: Rob McManus, *Gangs and Crime in South Carolina: How Much: How Bad?* December 9, 2009. http://thetandd.com.

- The National Youth Violence Prevention Resource Center states that most youth gang members are between the ages of **12 and 24**, with the average age 17 to 18 years.

- The U.S. Department of Justice states that gang members are the primary **retail-level distributors** of most illicit drugs.

Why Do Young People Join Gangs?

> 66All of these gangs prey on our children. They use children for their most dangerous and violent acts. They prey on their innocence, on their education, and on their lack of alternatives.99
>
> —Kathleen M. Rice, district attorney for Nassau County in Long Island, New York.

> 66The public is scandalized each time it is reported that gangs are recruiting children. Yet ganging has always been an adolescent pursuit—a developmental phase through which many youths pass on their way to adulthood.99
>
> —Judith Greene and Kevin Pranis, criminal justice policy analysts.

Psychologists, social workers, law enforcement professionals, and others who study gangs have theories about why young people join them. But no single factor or set of factors can accurately predict which youth will choose to become gang members. During 2007, students at a high school in Kansas City, Missouri, were asked to share their opinions about why kids join gangs. Some of the reasons given were protection from the dangers of the street, access to illegal drugs, and feelings of belonging to a family. Another reason given was that many young people have parents, uncles, cousins, siblings, or other relatives who belong to gangs, and some of them choose to follow in their relatives' footsteps.

A Substitute for Family

One of the most common reasons young people give for joining gangs is the desire to belong to a family-like group in the absence of that sort of closeness at home. This most often happens during the adolescent years, a vulnerable time when kids have an especially crucial need for guidance, love, and support. If their needs are not met by their families, they may look to gangs to fill the void. Psychiatrist Keith Ablow explains: "The studies have shown that gang members—kids who join gangs—often come from really dysfunctional, emotionally . . . challenged families."[32]

This was the case with Dashaun Morris, who writes about his past gang affiliation in a book entitled *War of the Bloods in My Veins*. Morris initially turned to gang life to escape from a home environment that he found unbearable. He had never known his father, and he hardly saw his mother because she worked at two or three different jobs. When he was nine years old, times became so difficult that his mother sent Morris from his home in New Jersey to live with his aunt and uncle in Phoenix, Arizona. In their cold, strict household, he felt neither loved nor wanted and was "completely miserable." He writes: "Every day it becomes harder to deal with being in the house and my spirit is regularly beaten down. Missing my mother and feeling like I have no family, my sadness makes me wonder if I'm worthy of being loved at all."[33] Yet as hard as family life was for Morris, his despondency began to lessen when he made friends with a boy called Ammo.

> **One of the most common reasons young people give for joining gangs is the desire to belong to a family-like group in the absence of having that sort of closeness at home.**

Morris, who had no prior experience with gangs, learned that Ammo was involved with the Bloods gang. He and his friends talked in gangster jargon that Morris did not understand, used peculiar hand signs, and always dressed in red clothing—never blue, which Ammo explained was forbidden because it was the color worn by their reviled enemy, the Crips. Eventually Morris came to understand the way they talked and dressed. He was also educated about all the different gangs in the city and the territories where they roamed. Even though the gang ways frightened him, Morris decided that he wanted to be a Blood too. "My adjustment to the gang is slow and I still don't quite fit in," he writes. "But if I want to have any sense of family and brothers who are down for me, I have to make this work. At times I want to lock myself within a padded room because of the fear I feel when I'm around them. To Ammo, I'm cool, but the other boys treat me like an outcast."[34] The other gang members eventually accepted Morris, and he became much more comfortable around them.

A year later Morris developed a close friendship with a classmate named Tray, whose six brothers were all Bloods. After school he often

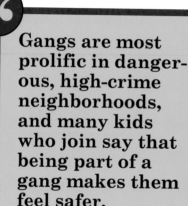

Gangs are most prolific in dangerous, high-crime neighborhoods, and many kids who join say that being part of a gang makes them feel safer.

hung out at Tray's house, where he learned more about gangs and their lifestyle of fighting, stealing, dealing drugs, and using guns to retaliate against the Crips. At the age of 11, Morris received his first assignment as a gang member: He was going to be taken for a drive, and they were heading for Crips territory. When they arrived, a gun was placed in his hands and he was ordered to point it at the men on the corner and start shooting—which he did.

Feeling a strange mix of horror and exhilaration, Morris watched as one body after another crumpled to the ground. He writes: "In the darkness of the streets, my childhood is murdered; innocence is shot. Yet, in the dawn of a new nightmare I am resurrected with earned power and respect. I am reborn—a gangster."[35] Afterward, Morris was officially declared a Blood. And although his conscience ached because of what he had done, his affiliation with the Bloods gave him a sense of security and belonging that he had never felt before. "There's nothing like the brotherhood," he writes, "especially when family is what you crave. . . . I'm unmotivated, depressed, fatherless, without direction or guidance, but I feel love from my new family.

We do everything together. Fight, protect, and fill voids that we can't get from home."[36]

The Protection Factor

Gangs are most prolific in dangerous, high-crime neighborhoods, and many kids who join say that being part of a gang makes them feel safer. Sometimes they think they have no choice, as rival gangs roam the streets and attempt to force young people into joining one or the other. Many gangs use fear and intimidation toward nonmembers, which can compel kids to join. As Mark Salazar, a former gang member who spent eight years in prison, explains: "Many times they join a gang as a sense of security and protection. If they're not affiliated with some group, they're on their own."[37]

A December 2007 question on an online forum elicited a response from someone who confirmed that safety was indeed a factor in why kids join gangs. Posting anonymously, he said that he had spent many years as part of a gang, had been shot six times, and had watched many of his childhood friends get killed or go to prison for the rest of their lives. Now a college graduate, he counsels youngsters about the dangers of gang life, and he shares his thoughts about why kids become involved with gangs:

> There are several reasons why, and they are different for each person. Yes, people join gangs to gain a sense of belonging, pride, power, etc. But there are also a lot of people who join a gang out of necessity. They grow up in an area that may be infested with gangs, causing them to walk through different gang territories on the way to school. Then those gangs start hurting them because of where they live, which is probably in their rivals' territory. They begin to get beat up, threatened, etc., finally turning to the gang where they live for help.[38]

Even though kids may feel safer as part of a gang, their risk of being assaulted or killed is much higher than if they were not in a gang. Chris Melde, who is a criminology professor at Michigan State University, researched this during a two-year project whose results he published in June 2009. Melde and his colleagues studied 1,450 students in the sixth through ninth grades from public schools in Arizona, New Mexico,

Massachusetts, and South Carolina. The students who joined gangs said that it made them feel safer even though they were victims of crime more often than their non-gang peers.

Child Gangsters

Some kids are born into families of gang members and are "blessed" into the gang when they are still babies. According to a June 2008 article in the *New York Daily News*, the children are dressed in gang colors, such as red for the Bloods and blue for the Crips, and taught to fold their fingers into gang signs before they are able to talk. "We're seeing more children who are being exposed to the gang world because their parents are members," says Deanna Rodriguez, gang bureau chief in the Brooklyn, New York, district attorney's office. "This is part of their identity. As long as they can remember, they've been part of the Bloods, Crips or the Latin Kings. This is what life is and they don't understand the concept of what life is outside that."[39]

Children who are blessed into gangs often go through what is known as a christening, which takes place during a church service. The priest holds them up toward the sun while people in the congregation say their prayers. Reverend Luis Barrios, who is an Episcopal priest and a professor at the John Jay College of Criminal Justice, has blessed about 300 children into the Association Neta and Latin Kings gangs, and he says that he sees nothing wrong with the ceremony. "It's not a criminal organization," he says. "It's a street organization with the capacity to bring together young people in search of power, collective identity . . . [and] belonging in the society that's rejecting them."[40]

> Some kids are born into families of gang members and are 'blessed' into the gang when they are still babies.

Many law enforcement officials vehemently disagree with Barrios's point of view. They argue that blessing children into gangs perpetuates a vicious cycle, with each new generation likely to adopt the violent gang lifestyle of the previous generation. Andrew Grascia, who is president of the New York State Gang Investigators, says that kids who grow up with gang parents are more likely to become bullies at a young age. "No child is born evil," he says. "They're taught evil things. You're taking a young, very fragile child who's being taught crime by the people who are supposed to secure and take care of him"[41]

Jonathan Jackson exemplifies Grascia's philosophy about children who are introduced to evil acts at an early age and grow up in a gang environment. Jackson, who is from Lauderhill, Florida, was blessed into the Crips at the age of eight because his father was a high-ranking member. He became immersed in the gang lifestyle, committing multiple crimes throughout the years. One of his most violent crime sprees occurred on Thanksgiving in 2008, when he and four other gang members robbed a series of Dunkin' Donuts stores. They forced people to the floor and began shooting at random. Six people were seriously wounded, one of whom was an 84-year-old veteran of World War II who was shot in the face. According to police, the men were shockingly casual about the crime—as though it were sport for them. "These are just cold-blooded thugs," says Sheriff Al Lamberti. "One suspect said he just wanted to up his body count."[42]

> " No one knows for sure how much control the gene variation has on a person's decision to join a gang, but many suspect that the answer lies in a combination of genetics and environment. "

The Genetic Connection

People who have an in-depth understanding of gangs and the gang lifestyle say that young people join gangs for a combination of reasons, such as living in a gang-infested neighborhood combined with an unsupportive family environment. But some studies have indicated that another factor may be involved: genetics. Since the 1990s research has suggested a link between aggressiveness and violent behavior in boys and the presence of a variation of a gene that controls an enzyme known as monoamine oxidase A (MAO-A), sometimes referred to as the "warrior gene." Low levels of MAO-A have been shown to result in an excessive breakdown of brain chemicals such as serotonin, which helps to regulate mood and emotions.

In June 2009 researchers from Florida State University took previous studies to a new level. They announced that boys who have low levels of MAO-A are more likely to join gangs, be especially violent, and be the gang members who are most likely to use weapons. No one knows for sure how much control the gene variation has on a person's decision to join a gang, but many suspect that the answer lies in a combination of genetics and environment. Joshua Buckholtz, who is a neuroscience PhD candidate at Vanderbilt University's Brain Institute and Department of Psychology explains: "What all these risk gene studies show us is that genes do an important job in loading the gun. But it's the environment that pulls the trigger."[43]

No Simple Answers

Why some young people make the choice to join gangs and so many others refrain from doing so is puzzling to everyone who studies gangs. A number of factors have been identified, including the search for a family-like group of friends, protection from the dangers of the streets, growing up in a gang environment and knowing nothing else, and genetics. If more definitive reasons are discovered, at-risk youth may eventually be targeted and convinced to stay out of gangs—long before they make the decision to embark on a life of crime and violence.

Why Do Young People Join Gangs?

66 While it is contrary to the theories of social scientists, who persist in attributing poverty and despair as the leading cause driving young people into gangs, the ultimate roadblock to a gang is a stable family. 99

—Tony Rafael, *The Mexican Mafia*. New York: Encounter, 2007, p. 362.

Rafael is a writer from Los Angeles who has researched gangs for more than 10 years.

....

66 Latino communities around the country are full of at-risk youths with little parental supervision and a lack of love and acceptance at home. Turning to the street, these children find the love and acceptance they seek in a street gang—until they wind up in prison, in a hospital, or dead. 99

—Samuel Logan, *This Is for the Mara Salvatrucha: Inside the MS-13, America's Most Violent Gang*. New York: Hyperion, 2009, p. 244.

Logan, an investigative reporter based in Brazil, reports on gang activity throughout the United States, Mexico, and Central America.

....

Bracketed quotes indicate conflicting positions.

* Editor's Note: While the definition of a primary source can be narrowly or broadly defined, for the purposes of Compact Research, a primary source consists of: 1) results of original research presented by an organization or researcher; 2) eyewitness accounts of events, personal experience, or work experience; 3) first-person editorials offering pundits' opinions; 4) government officials presenting political plans and/or policies; 5) representatives of organizations presenting testimony or policy.

Primary Source Quotes

66 Many Asian youth gangs may start out as just a social group of friends and acquaintances. But more commonly, larger and more established gangs actively recruit new members into the gang. Once the new member finds a sense of belonging and acceptance . . . it's often very hard for him/her to give it up. 99

—C.N. Le, "Asian American Gangs," *Asian-Nation: The Landscape of Asian America*, January 24, 2010. www.asian-nation.org.

Le holds a PhD in sociology and is the creator and author of the *Asian-Nation* Web site.

66 While we wonder why some join gangs, we need to acknowledge that gangs offer a perception of short-term benefit: a sense of security to a kid who feels threatened, a sense of belonging to a kid who feels adrift, and a sense of risk to young people wanting to show their independence. 99

—Steven D. Strachan, "Four Myths That Complicate Efforts to Confront Gang Violence," *Seattle Times*, January 29, 2009. http://seattletimes.nwsource.com.

Strachan is chief of police in Kent, Washington.

66 Kids who live in an area that is already overrun with gangs and who are subjected to gang violence often join gangs in an attempt to obtain safety and protection from the violence. 99

—Gerald L. Zahorchak, testimony, Senate Judiciary Hearing, National Constitution Center, February 19, 2007. http://judiciary.senate.gov.

Zahorchak is Pennsylvania's secretary of education.

66 Sometimes, membership in a certain gang is a family tradition. Kids join the gang that their father, brother or cousins joined before them. 99

—Sarah Hammond, "Gang Busters," National Conference of State Legislatures (NCSL), June 2008. www.ncsl.org.

Hammond specializes in juvenile justice issues for the NCSL.

❝Prisons in the United States and Central America give new and existing gang members the opportunity to network and hone their skills, and have been dubbed 'gangland finishing schools.' In addition, new and unaffiliated inmates may have little choice but to join a gang.❞

—Jessica M. Vaughan and John D. Feere, "Taking Back the Streets: ICE and Local Law Enforcement Target Immigrant Gangs," *Backgrounder*, Center for Immigration Studies, October 2008. www.cis.org.

Vaughan and Feere are policy analysts with the Center for Immigration Studies.

....

❝Most children who are drawn to gangs do so out of a need to affiliate and connect. They 'age out' of this interest quickly and move on to more healthy activities and concerns on their own.❞

—Charles J. Ogletree Jr., *Addressing Gangs: What's Effective? What's Not?* Testimony before the House Subcommittee on Crime, Terrorism, and Homeland Security, June 10, 2008. http://judiciary.house.gov.

Ogletree is a law professor at Harvard Law School and the founder of the Charles Hamilton Houston Institute for Race & Justice.

....

❝The 13-year old kids getting recruited into gangs need us to stand up and fight for them.❞

—John S. Pistole, "2nd Los Angeles IACP Summit on Transnational Gangs, Los Angeles, California," *Major Executive Speeches*, Federal Bureau of Investigation, March 3, 2008. www.fbi.gov.

Pistole is deputy director of the Federal Bureau of Investigation.

....

❝Juveniles with a history of delinquency are more likely to join gangs and, once in the gang, to engage in higher rates of criminal activity than they would have otherwise.❞

—David B. Muhlhausen, *The Youth PROMISE Act: Outside the Scope and Expertise of the Federal Government*, testimony before the Committee on the Judiciary, Subcommittee on Crime, Terrorism, and Homeland Security of the United States House of Representatives, July 15, 2009. www.heritage.org.

Muhlhausen is a senior policy analyst at the Heritage Foundation's Center for Data Analysis.

....

Why Do Young People Join Gangs?

- A 2009 study by criminal justice professor Chris Melde found that most youth who join gangs do so in order to **feel safer**.

- Social psychologist Malcolm Klein states that only about **15 percent** of young people in a given neighborhood choose to join gangs.

- According to the National Youth Violence Prevention Resource Center, one 11-city survey of eighth graders found that **38 percent** of gang members were female, and female gang members are generally younger than male gang members.

- The National Youth Violence Prevention Resource Center states that **few teenagers are forced** to join gangs and most can refuse to join without fear of retaliation.

- After analyzing gang involvement over a two-year period, criminal justice professor Chris Melde found that students who joined gangs had higher levels of **victimization** but at the same time reported a relatively large **decrease in fear**.

- According to a July 2007 report by the Justice Policy Institute, the most powerful factors that deter kids from joining gangs are **education-related**, including commitment to school, attachment to teachers, and parents' expectations for school.

Common Risk Factors

Those who study gangs and gang activity say there is no one factor or group of factors that influence kids to join gangs. But according the the group Operation No Gangs, a number of risk factors for youth have been identified.

Thirteen risk factors for gang membership*
Low-income minority male, aged 12 to 16
Household run by single parent
Father uninvolved in child's life, dysfunctional as a parent, or incarcerated
Child not accustomed to following rules or consistent family expectations
English not the primary language in the home/Recent immigrant
Deficient reading skills
Poor academic performer/Learning and/or emotional disabilities/ Attention span deficiency
Poor verbal communication skills
Low self-esteem/Exhibits traits of a follower
Poor anger control, impulse control, and conflict resolution skills
By age 15, has exhibited difficulty associating actions with consequences
Has developed discipline problems in school and in the neighborhood
Has exhibited a trend toward near-exclusive alliance with friends who serve as "second family"

*Note: Youth with five or more factors are considered high-risk for becoming involved with gangs.

Source: Operation No Gangs, Hispanic Youth Gang Affiliation Candidate Profile, 2007. http://operationnogangs.org.

- The Violence Prevention Institute states that gang activity offers a **sense of security** for young people whose home environment lacks a close family structure.

- A study released in June 2009 by researchers from Florida State University showed that males with a low level of activity on a gene that codes an enzyme known as **MAO-A** were nearly twice as likely to join a gang than males with the high-activity gene, and were nearly twice as likely to use weapons and violence during a fight.

Gangs and Drug Trafficking

According to the January 2009 report *National Gang Threat Assessment 2009*, gang members are the primary retail-level distributors of most illicit drugs. This graph shows the percentage of U.S. law enforcement agencies who reported gang involvement by drug type from 2004 to 2008.

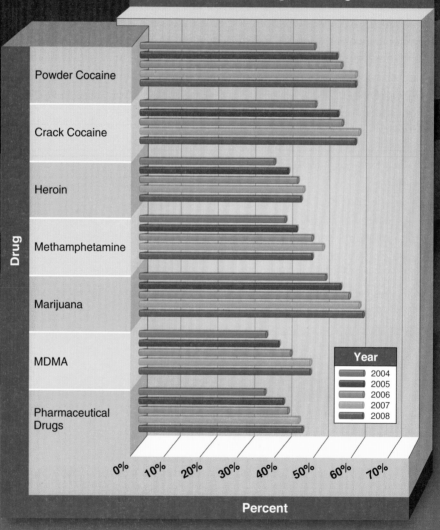

U.S. Law Enforcement Agencies Reporting Gang Involvement in Illicit Drug Trafficking 2004 to 2008

Source: National Gang Intelligence Center and National Drug Intelligence Center, *National Gang Threat Assessment 2009*, January 2009. www.justice.gov.

- According to a July 2007 report by the Justice Policy Institute, no **single factor** or **set of factors** can successfully predict which young people will become gang members.

- The U.S. Department of Justice states that gangs are increasingly enticing young people to join gangs by **recruiting them on the Internet.**

- According to social psychologist Malcolm Klein, factors that cause young people to join gangs include **poor parenting, justifying delinquent behavior**, and **traumatic events** in their lives.

- In August 2009 law enforcement officials in Miami-Dade and Broward counties in Florida reported that the stresses caused by the **poor economy** play a role in kids joining gangs.

Can People Leave the Gang Life Behind?

66 **Research has documented that former gang members, especially marginal and short-term ones, typically left a gang without complication or facing any serious consequences.** 99

—James C. Howell, Arlen Egley Jr., and Christina O'Donnell, research associates with the National Gang Center.

66 **Being 'jumped out' of the gang may appear to be the only way to get out of certain gangs, but one never knows the danger that one might find in receiving his beating to get out. A lot of gangs don't want anyone leaving.** 99

—Rob Gallardo, director of Operation No Gangs, an organization that presents seminars to educate people about gangs.

C had (not his real name) is a teenager who had his first experience with a gang when he was six and was coaxed into the Folk Nation by his older brother. His initiation involved slap-boxing, whereby gang members slapped him over and over again. When Chad decided to become an active member at the age of 12, he faced a far more serious initiation—walking by a line of 25 gang members who could injure him in most any way they chose. "They couldn't cut me or shoot me," he says, "but they could hit me with whatever they wanted to. If they wanted to hit you with a 2 × 4 or tire iron, they could. If you fell down more than four times, they killed you."[44]

After moving from southern Florida to Anderson, South Carolina, Chad started a branch (known as a set) of Folk Nation there. But as time went by, he began to realize that the gang life was not what he wanted for himself. He grew tired of being involved in crime and constantly feeling scared that gangbangers would break into his house or hurt him or his family. "When you first get in the gang, you love it," he says. "But it's a living hell when you get in. It ain't fun when you're doing stuff illegal and you got to watch over your shoulder all the time." Although Chad is still officially a member of Folk Nation, he is no longer involved in gang activities. But there is no guarantee that he will be allowed to remain un-involved, as he explains: "I will always be a member. I'm not active right now, but if I am called up and asked to do a mission, I have to do it. If I don't, they'll kill me."[45]

Quitting a Gang—the Hard Way

Those who study gangs say that whether people are allowed to leave largely depends on the gang itself and the rules that members agree to when they join. Alex Alonso, a well-known historian and researcher who specializes in gang life, says he often hears from "naïve outsiders" that members can never leave the gang without living in constant fear for their lives. Alonso insists that this is a "Hollywood myth" fueled by irresponsible journalism, and is "capped off by exaggerated law enforcement reports based on their anecdotal experiences." He writes: "Leaving a gang is not a treasonous act and teenagers walk away from the gang often."[46]

Yet based on personal stories shared by many gang members, not all gangs adhere to the philosophy described by Alonso. A former gangbanger named José says it is not uncommon for members to be told that they cannot ever leave the gang. Even if they are allowed to quit, they are often required to be "jumped out," meaning they must undergo a beating by gang members. Alonso refers to this as a "brief assault to serve as a penalty,"[47] but according to José, the jumping out process

> " Even if they are allowed to quit, they are often required to be 'jumped out,' meaning they must undergo a beating by gang members. "

can be brutal. He says that in addition to being beaten bloody, someone who wants to leave the gang may be stabbed by gang members.

Ricky Le is a former gangbanger whose exit could hardly be described as a "brief assault"—in fact, quitting nearly cost him his life. Le belonged to a Lowell, Massachusetts, gang called the Moonlight Strangers. At the age of 15 he made the decision to leave the gang life behind, and he knew that his only option was to be jumped out. He was well aware of the risks involved, as he explains: "The rule is, anything goes. They could use weapons, they could have 50 people—anything goes."[48] After Le and 20 gang members climbed to the top of a hill, he cringed as he watched the beating of 15-year-old Paul Som, another boy who wanted to leave the gang. One gangbanger after another took his turn, brutally beating Som in the head with a combination lock wrapped in a cloth. As vicious as Som's beating was, though, Le knew that his punishment would be worse because he was going last.

> "One gang that is notorious for forbidding its members to quit is the Mara Salvatrucha."

Finally the violent group turned on Le. They ruthlessly punched him with their fists, kicked him in the head, and beat him with crowbars. He remembers little about the attack, however, because he was so badly injured that he was knocked unconscious. When he woke up in the hospital two weeks later, Le felt as though he were peering through a net with his family on the other side, and he saw that his sister was crying. He learned that he had sustained a traumatic brain injury and had been in a coma the entire time. "I couldn't eat or walk," he says. "I was in a wheelchair for a month, and then it was changed to a walker."[49] Although Le's injuries were life-threatening, he slowly recovered. Today, because of all that he went through, he helps educate young people about the risks and dangers of being involved with gangs.

When Death Is the Only Option

One gang that is notorious for forbidding its members to quit is the Mara Salvatrucha. In fact, new recruits are informed up front that no one is ever allowed to leave because quitting is considered an insult and a sign of disloyalty. Kellene Bishop, an emergency preparedness consultant who teaches people how to defend themselves against gangs and other threats, explains: "Once a member is brought into the gang, they are in for life. They cannot act without the boss's consent—they cannot kill without reason, cannot talk to the police, cannot skip gang meetings, nor can they leave the gang. MS-13 has no tolerance for gang members who drop out. A MS-13 member and even their family members must die in order to exit MS-13, no exceptions."[50]

Bishop cites the example of Ernesto Miranda. An illegal alien who was one of the original founders of MS-13, Miranda served as one of the gang's high-ranking soldiers. After he was deported from the United States back to his native El Salvador, he was determined to leave the gang life behind and turn his life around. He was a devoted father who was studying law and aspired to work with children to help keep them out of gangs. But Miranda was never able to achieve his goals. In May 2006, MS-13 members showed up at his home and shot him to death as punishment for turning his back on them.

> " Those who are members of certain prison gangs also face danger if they try to quit. This is especially true of the Mexican Mafia and Aryan Brotherhood, both of which have a creed called 'Blood in, blood out.' "

Another gang member who wanted to quit the MS-13 was Edgar Chocoy, a teenager from Villanueva, Guatemala. At the age of 14, Chocoy knew that this had led to his being "green lighted," meaning marked for death by gang members. He hid out with relatives until it became too dangerous for them, then traveled by bus to Mexico and illegally crossed the U.S. border. He was eventually discovered by immigration officials and sent to a detention camp in Colorado where illegal aliens were held. It was there that he learned about asylum laws, which are based on the concept that people should not be returned to countries where their life or freedom may be threatened. Chocoy was hopeful that such laws would protect him by allowing him to stay in the United States.

Appearing before a judge, Chocoy pleaded not to be sent back to Guatemala. He wrote in an affidavit: "I am certain that if I had stayed in Guatemala the members of the gang MS would have killed me. I have seen them beat people up with baseball bats and rocks and shoot at them. I know they kill people. I know they torture people . . . I know that if I am returned to Guatemala I will be tortured by them. I know that they will kill me if I am returned to Guatemala. They will kill me because I left their gang."[51] The judge, however, did not grant the request, and on March 10, 2004, Chocoy was deported back to his native country. Knowing that he was in grave danger, he hid in his aunt's home for two and a half weeks. When he finally felt that it was safe to venture outside, he was gunned down in the street and killed.

> " In some cases people who have quit gangs have had to move away from their homes or cities in order to protect themselves and their families. "

Those who are members of certain prison gangs also face danger if they try to quit. This is especially true of the Mexican Mafia and Aryan Brotherhood, both of which have a creed called "Blood in, blood out." In order to be initiated into these gangs, potential members are required to shed someone's blood (known as "blood in"), typically by killing a member of a rival prison gang. Once they are accepted into the gang, their membership is considered to be permanent—the only way out is to die. Robert Walker, a former agent with the U.S. Drug Enforcement Administration who now serves as a gang identification consultant, explains: "Most prison gang members are expected to remain members for life. Even if released from prison they are expected to remain loyal to the incarcerated members by providing support to them, by whatever means, usually through the proceeds of drug sales and/or other street crimes. The penalty for 'quitting' the gang is death; In other words 'Blood out.'"[52]

Running for Their Lives

Michelle Arciaga, who is a senior research associate with the National Gang Center, says that many gang members make the conscious decision to leave the gang lifestyle and succeed in doing so. She writes: "It IS easier to get into a gang than to get out of one, but you can choose to leave the gang life today."[53] Arciaga acknowledges, however, that in some cases people who have quit gangs have had to move away from their homes or cities in order to protect themselves and their families. Although no statistics have been compiled on the number of gang members who have been relocated, experts say that such relocations happen in communities throughout the United States.

Durham, North Carolina, pastor Kenneth Hammond has helped several young people escape the gang life, and he says he would not hesitate to do it again. He explains: "We've been involved with a number of tragedies here. Sometimes, there is just too much danger to keep them here."[54] One person he helped relocate was a 15-year-old boy whose life had been threatened for wanting to quit the gang. Hammond secretly made arrangements to move him and his family to a town in Ohio located more than 400 miles (644km) away. The same is true of other pastors in Durham, who have provided assistance to former gang members in order to give them a fresh start in a new location.

John Reis, a former gang investigator from Rhode Island, has also been involved in the relocation of young people who want to leave gangs. He says that the point is to provide them with a change of scenery in the hope that they will take measures to change their lives for the better. In 2001 Reis secretly helped a 16-year-old Latin Kings member from Providence, Rhode Island, relocate to New York City. "You are dealing with a kid's life here," he says. "If you don't do something, they could end up dead tomorrow."[55]

Although some gangs allow members to leave, others forbid it and expect a lifetime commitment. Of those who do manage to walk away from a gang, many must endure vicious beatings by gang members—and even if they survive, many continue to live in fear for themselves and their families. An anonymous former gang member posted in an online forum that he spent many years in a gang and was shot six times. He eventually quit, but he says that his violent past will haunt him for the rest of his life. He writes: "The point is, even though you may be fortunate enough to get out or get away at some point in your life, you never REALLY get away. The psychological damage caused by the years of gang banging you took part in will NEVER go away. The emotional scars, along with the physical scars, will be there forever."[56]

Can People Leave
the Gang Life Behind?

> 66 Leaving the gang early reduces the risk of negative life outcomes, but current [law enforcement] policies make it more difficult for gang members to quit. 99

—Judith Greene and Kevin Pranis, *Gang Wars: The Failure of Enforcement Tactics and the Need for Effective Safety Strategies*, Justice Policy Institute, July 2007. www.justicepolicy.org.

Greene and Pranis are criminal justice policy analysts.

> 66 Do law enforcement officers and school officials make it harder for youth to quit gangs? Given all the many programs, both national and regional throughout the nation, that police departments and educators participate in trying to keep youth away from gangs, this comment seems ridiculous and is not based on any fact. 99

—Know Gangs, "Separating Fact from Fiction: The Truth Behind the Justice Policy Institute Report," July 1, 2007. www.knowgangs.com.

Know Gangs provides training to law enforcement personnel, educators, and social service workers to educate them about gangs, drugs, and school violence.

Bracketed quotes indicate conflicting positions.

* Editor's Note: While the definition of a primary source can be narrowly or broadly defined, for the purposes of Compact Research, a primary source consists of: 1) results of original research presented by an organization or researcher; 2) eyewitness accounts of events, personal experience, or work experience; 3) first-person editorials offering pundits' opinions; 4) government officials presenting political plans and/or policies; 5) representatives of organizations presenting testimony or policy.

66 **The most dangerous method of leaving a gang usually comes after law enforcement has put enormous pressure on a suspect or defendant to reveal information, and intelligence. That's where the danger of leaving a gang comes from.** 99

—Alex Alonso, "Departing from the Gang Can Be Easy," Street Gangs Resource Center, August 23, 2009. www.streetgangs.com.

Alonso is a well-known historian and researcher who specializes in gang life.

....

66 **Gang members decide to leave the gang lifestyle every day in cities around the U.S. It is a myth that the only way to leave a gang is by dying.** 99

—Michelle Arciaga, "Common Myths About Gangs," East Coast Gang Investigators Association, February 23, 2009. www.gripe4rkids.org.

Arciaga is a senior research associate at the National Gang Center.

....

66 **Once a member of MS-13, it is difficult to leave because leaving the gang is considered an insult and an act of disloyalty. A gang member who has left the gang often still bears identifying tattoos and faces the possibility that he will cross paths with someone who will uphold the MS-13 'honor code' by killing him.** 99

—Jessica M. Vaughan and John D. Feere, "Taking Back the Streets: ICE and Local Law Enforcement Target Immigrant Gangs," *Backgrounder*, Center for Immigration Studies, October 2008. www.cis.org.

Vaughan and Feere are policy analysts with the Center for Immigration Studies.

....

66 When I am released, I am going to have nothing to do with the people from my past life. A lot of them will probably have problems with me 'cause I have no loyalty toward them no more, but one day I'm going to have to face that—and when that time comes, I'm not really sure what I will do. All I really can do is face it like a man. 99

—Ted Braden, "My Biggest Regret," Teen in Jail, September 1, 2009. www.teeninjail.com.

Braden, a former gang member who was convicted of drug trafficking, is a prisoner at Lancaster Work Camp in Trenton, Florida.

66 The truth is, they're able to leave the gang just as easily as they arrived. The path from jumping in to the moment they gain the courage to remove themselves from the gang, however, is fraught with criminal behavior. 99

—Samuel Logan, *This Is for the Mara Salvatrucha*. New York: Hyperion, 2009, p. 244.

Logan, an investigative reporter based in Brazil, reports on gang activity throughout the United States, Mexico, and Central America.

66 Do you ever wonder why you don't see very many old gang bangers out messing around? I don't. They're all either dead or in prison. 99

—Anonymous, response to "Why Do You Think People Join Gangs? Have You Ever Been in a Gang?" AnswerBag, December 9, 2007. www.answerbag.com.

This online post is by a man who says he spent many years in a gang and was shot six times before he finally decided to leave the gang life behind.

Facts and Illustrations

Can People Leave the Gang Life Behind?

- The National Youth Violence Prevention Resource Center states that **one-half to two-thirds** of gang members leave after one year.

- According to a July 2007 report by the Justice Policy Institute, data from national and local youth surveys indicate that the typical gang member is active for **a year or less**.

- The U.S. Department of Education states that people who want to leave a gang should **never tell other gang members** about their intentions because the risk of retaliation is so high.

- According to Rob Gallardo, the director of Operation No Gangs, the earlier someone chooses to get out of a gang, the better his or her **chances for success**.

- A July 2007 report by the Justice Policy Institute states that most people who leave gangs do so because they either **grow out of it** or they no longer want the **violent lifestyle**.

- Gabriel Hinojos, who joined the gang Florencia 13 when he was 14 years old, says that some people are allowed to leave gangs if they have **served time in prison**.

- Each year the organization Homeboy Industries helps about **8,000** young men and women leave gangs, but not all of them stay out permanently.

Reasons People Quit Gangs

Whether gang members are allowed to quit generally depends on the individual gang and the rules members agree to when they join. This table shows some of the most common reasons people give for leaving the gang life behind.

Reason for leaving
Difficulty finding a position within a gang
Inability to get along with higher ranking members
Strengthened family relationships steered them away from the gang
Moved to a new neighborhood/New town
Maturity—marriage, children, education, stable job
Turned off by the gang culture in general
Tired of violent lifestyle/Committing crimes
Incarceration

Sources: Alex Alonso, "Departing from the Gang Can Be Easy," Street Gangs, August 23, 2009. www.streetgangs.com; Judith Greene and Kevin Pranis, *Gang Wars: The Failure of Enforcement Tactics and the Need for Effective Strategies*, July 2007. www.justicepolicy.org.

- In a 2009 interview with American RadioWorks, a former member of a Latino gang said that the biggest hurdle for people who want to leave gangs is their **pride**—gang members will berate them, calling them cowards and punks.

- According to noted gang expert Alex Alonso, an extremely common form of allowing a member to leave a gang is known as **"jumping out,"** whereby the person is assaulted by gang members as a penalty.

- Arturo Hernandez, who is an educator, counselor, and expert on youth gang involvement, says that all the former gang members he knows did not actually leave the gang, but they **stopped participating** in violent activities, drug sales, and theft.

Gang Membership Remains Steady

Many published articles discuss people who have quit gangs in order to change their lives for the better, but no statistics exist that can accurately depict how many have actually done so. Although gang membership has fluctuated throughout the years, according to yearly reports by the U.S. Department of Justice, from 1975 to 2007 the number of gang members rose more than 1,700 percent. This graph shows the year-to-year changes in gang membership.

Estimated number of gang members in the United States – 1975 to 2007

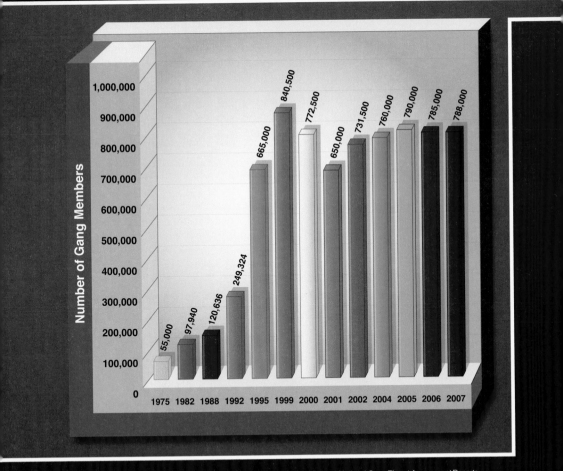

Source: National Gang Intelligence Center and National Drug Intelligence Center, *National Gang Threat Assessment* Reports, 1995–2009, January 2009. www.justice.gov.

Support Programs

For some people, once they have joined a gang it is difficult to get out, either because of the gang's rules about lifetime membership or an overall lack of direction in their lives. To address this need, a number of programs have been implemented throughout the United States to keep young people out of gangs and help those who want to leave the gang life behind. This table shows four of the programs that have proven to be successful.

Program	Services Provided
Homeboy Industries Los Angeles	Serves gang members and former gang members by providing job training and placement, mental health counseling, legal services, education classes, and tattoo removal. Also provides on-site employment at its six different businesses.
Project 180 Bakersfield, CA	Works to connect at-risk students with the services they need, such as before- and after-school tutoring, leadership training, substance abuse treatment, career training, community service, and positive, healthy activities, as well as tattoo removal and assistance for young people who want to leave gangs.
Council for Unity New York City	Former gang members work with young people in school, out of school, and at correctional facilities to provide them with support and hope for the future, increase their self-confidence, and encourage them to leave gangs and violence behind.
Ceasefire Chicago	Outreach workers, most of whom are former gang members, work with youth to keep them out of trouble, including involving them in activities, assisting them in finding jobs or educational opportunities, helping those who are on drugs to get into treatment programs, and mediating disputes.

Sources: Homeboy Industries, "Programs and Services: Overview," 2008. www.homeboy-industries.org; Kern County Project 180, *Is Your Child Heading Down the Wrong Path?* 2007. www.static.kern.org; Council for Unity, "Our Programs, Products, and Services," 2008. www.councilforunity.org; CeaseFire, *The Campaign to Stop the Shooting.* www.ceasefirechicago.org.

- The Justice Policy Institute states that leaving a gang is associated with a significant **reduction in delinquent activity**.

Can Gang Violence Be Stopped?

❝It is critical that Congress pass a comprehensive gang bill which takes a multifaceted approach to addressing gang violence and activities. It must include a strong enforcement component, in addition to prevention and intervention measures.❞

—David A. Goad, president of the National Sheriffs' Association.

❝Violent street crime committed by gang members is a serious problem in many states. But turning crimes that are fundamentally local in nature into federal crimes is not the solution.❞

—Brian W. Walsh, senior research fellow at the Heritage Foundation's Center for Legal and Judicial Studies.

The steady growth of gangs and gang-related crime presents a formidable challenge for federal, state, and local law enforcement throughout the United States. Some evidence, however, suggests that progress has been made. For instance, since 1992 the FBI's Safe Streets Violent Crime Initiative has focused on the most violent gangs, crimes of violence, and the apprehension of violent fugitives. A key part of the program is the agency's 160 task forces, which are composed of more than 2,000 local, state, and federal investigators representing 653 law enforcement agencies. From 2001 to 2008 this endeavor resulted in over 40,000 arrests and nearly 17,000 convictions of gang members for criminal activities.

Such collaboration between law enforcement agencies has resulted in a marked reduction of crime in Aurora, Illinois. During the 1990s Aurora was a virtual war zone, with hundreds of gang-related shootings and an estimated two dozen murders committed each year. Police Chief Greg Thomas explains: "It became so routine. It was shooting after shooting after shooting with no way to break the cycle."[57] In the years since, federal agents have partnered with local law enforcement officials to focus on Aurora's most violent gangs. In the process they have captured dozens of gang leaders to get them off the streets and dismantle their operations. This collaborative effort has resulted in a dramatic decline in the city's murder rate. During 2008, for example, only two homicides were reported, and fewer than 100 shootings occurred—down from 354 in 1996.

A Proven Success

A widely held belief among those who are knowledgeable about gangs is that gang violence cannot be viewed solely as a problem for law enforcement. Rather, it is a societal issue that is highly complex, involves a number of factors, and requires a multifaceted array of solutions. As the Web site Know Gangs states: "The gang problem needs to be recognized as a community problem, not a police problem. We need to address the gang problem at all levels—suppression, prevention and intervention."[58]

> **The steady growth of gangs and gang-related crime presents a formidable challenge for federal, state, and local law enforcement throughout the United States.**

This is the theory behind a program that was created by David Kennedy, who is a professor at New York City's John Jay College of Criminal Justice. Kennedy began to study gangs and gang activity during the 1980s, and in the process he collaborated with numerous criminologists and law enforcement professionals. He became aware that an overwhelmingly disproportionate number of violent crimes are committed by a small number of hardened criminals, a fact that is widely recognized among those who work in law enforcement. Kennedy also learned something that he found startling at first because of its simplicity. Arresting shooters or threatening them with imprisonment generally does not prevent homicides, but one tactic *is* effective: telling them to stop. Kennedy says gangbangers are informed that if they do not stop, "the consequences will be swift, and certain, and severe, and punishment will be handed out not just to the individual involved in the shooting but to everyone in the individual's gang."[59] With that as his basis, Kennedy developed a program known as Ceasefire.

Kennedy had already achieved success with Ceasefire in Boston when he proposed it to officials in Cincinnati during 2006. The city was clearly losing its battle against gangs, with murders and other violent crimes continuing to escalate at an alarming rate. In 2006 alone there were 89 homicides, the highest number on record. Kennedy outlined his program to city officials, and they decided to give it a try. Police officers analyzed crime records and compiled a list of gang members who were on parole or probation. Then a meeting known as a call-in was scheduled, and the people on the list were notified and compelled to attend.

> " A widely held belief among those who are knowledgeable about gangs is that gang violence cannot be viewed solely as a problem for law enforcement. "

About 30 men were at the call-in on July 31, 2007. They first heard from physician Vincent Garcia, who heads up the trauma unit at Cincinnati Children's Hospital. Garcia explained that on almost a daily basis he saw innocent children who were severely injured or killed while caught in the crossfire of gang fighting. He assured the men that he cared about them, and he knew they could do better than resort to a life of violence. Then Thomas Streicher, Cincinnati's chief of police, delivered a stern message: "We know who you are, we know who your friends are, and we know what you're doing. If your boys don't stop shooting people right now, we're coming after everyone in your group."[60] Other speakers followed, including an ex–gang member and his shooting victim, a woman who was left paralyzed and was confined to a wheelchair. At the meeting's close, the attendees were introduced to social workers who were available to help with job and educational assistance, and they were given an information packet with a phone number to call if they wanted help.

The Ceasefire program had a significant impact on gang violence in Cincinnati. At the end of 2007 the city's homicides were down 24 percent from the prior year—and by the following April, gang-related murders had dropped 50 percent. Streicher, who was initially skeptical of a crime-fighting program that was developed by a college professor, admitted how wrong he had been. "We will never engage in this kind of gang work again without academic support," he says. "No police department should."[61]

Getting to Kids Early

Among those who have studied gangs, there is an overwhelming consensus: The earlier young people are provided with support and educated about the dangers of gang life, the more likely they will be to stay away from gangs. A teenager named Donovan emphasized this in an October 2008 presentation to community leaders in Baltimore. He said that although many of his relatives and friends were Crips, he had personally resisted joining the gang. He shared his philosophy about gangs and the importance of reaching out to kids at an early age: "Gangs are like an incurable disease. You need to let go of the 11th and 12th graders. The disease got them. Quarantine them. Get to the young ones before they get too sick."[62]

> " **One program that has proved to be successful is known as Scared Straight, which involves rounding up kids and giving them a first-hand look at the harsh realities of gang life.** "

One program that has proved to be successful is known as Scared Straight, which involves rounding up kids and giving them a first-hand look at the harsh realities of gang life. The goal is for young people to be frightened enough by what they see and hear that they will turn away from gangs. As noted gang expert Sudhir Venkatesh writes: "Police will use a 'scared straight' approach by taking young people to the station where they frighten them with information about jail conditions, the possibility of being beaten up by imprisoned gang members, and so on. I know many parents who love it when police 'scare' their children into getting off the corner and back into school."[63]

In November 2009 police officers in Orange County, California, utilized the Scared Straight program with 67 teens who were on the street past curfew. After picking them up, the police drove them to headquarters, where they waited on jail buses for their parents to arrive. Later, the teens and their parents met with representatives of the district attorney's office and the probation department to discuss the possible consequences of being out past curfew. They were shown large poster boards covered with photos of young people who had all been killed while on the streets

> **Another concern many have about gang injunctions is that they violate rights granted under the First Amendment of the Constitution, which prohibits the government from abridging people's right to peacefully assemble.**

late at night, and the teens were asked if that was how they wanted to end up. "It's a very good thing if we get kids when they're young and we get them off the street," says District Attorney Tony Rackauckas. "Clearly they're not doing anything good if they're out there after 10 o'clock."[64]

The Gang Injunction Controversy

One method some communities use to fight gang violence is imposing anti-gang ordinances known as injunctions. The injunctions vary from city to city but in general they prohibit gang members from engaging in certain activities in clearly defined "safety zones." They may not associate with each other, display gang signs, wear gang colors, intimidate others or block their ability to pass, among other restrictions. If gang members violate any of these rules, they are subject to fines, jail time, or both.

In Los Angeles, law enforcement officials have implemented 37 injunctions that involve 57 gangs. According to the city's police department, the reason for such injunctions is to address the neighborhood gang problem "before it reaches the level of felony crime activity." The LAPD's Web site explains the benefits:

> Gang injunctions have a clearly demonstrable positive [effect] on the neighborhood area covered. Some have had a remarkable effect. In smaller areas, gang nuisance activity can be permanently removed. In larger areas, with gangs entrenched for years, the gang's hold on the area can be reduced and maintained with a small team of law enforcement officers. Anecdotal evidence is fully supportive; residents continue to ask for the period of peace a gang injunction can provide.[65]

Yet not everyone agrees that injunctions should be used as a deterrent to gangs. According to Venkatesh, one of the risks is that police do not always have a reliable way of determining who is in a gang and who is not. He writes: "In Chicago, for example, police department officials told me that 4 out of 5 youths are mistakenly believed to be gang members. In smaller cities . . . I am almost positive that the rate is much lower. However, police often do not have an effective way of figuring out whether someone is in a gang, so they round up many young people who have never had any involvement in gang activity."[66]

Another concern many have about gang injunctions is that they violate rights granted under the First Amendment of the Constitution, which prohibits the government from abridging people's right to peacefully assemble. In January 2009 the American Civil Liberties Union filed a lawsuit challenging a gang injunction that was proposed for a section of Los Angeles. In a news release, the group explains its opposition:

> Individuals under the proposed injunction would be subject to strict curfews, prohibited from associating with certain people, banned from the area's largest park and prevented from wearing "gang apparel," although the injunction never specifies what that is. The rules are so restrictive and cover such a large area—encompassing schools, churches and the homes of family members—that it would be nearly impossible for someone to comply without moving out of the area. [67]

A New Beginning

Father Greg Boyle, who is a priest in Los Angeles, has a unique philosophy about gangs: Their existence is not a crime issue but rather the result of societal breakdown and hopelessness. He explains: "You have to address the lethal absence of hope. I have never seen a hopeful person join a gang."[68] Boyle founded an organization known as Homeboy Industries during the 1980s. Since that time he has worked with thousands of gang members, some who have left their gangs and others who are still active. He provides them with a sense of family, gives them jobs, and helps them feel that there is hope for the future.

The people who participate in the Homeboy Industries program work at the organization's small businesses, which include Homeboy Bakery, Homegirl Café, Homeboy Silk Screen, Homeboy Maintenance, Homeboy Merchandise, and Homeboy Solar Panel Installers. All those who are employed earn a regular salary, with health care benefits after three months on the job. Boyle's goal is to introduce gang members to the discipline of being gainfully employed in the hope that they will eventually find jobs in the commercial sector.

Three men whose lives have been transformed because of Homeboy Industries are Rudolpho Marquez, Richard Reyes, and Cesar Cruz. Former gang rivals and ex-convicts, all three now work at the Homeboy solar panel installation business. Whereas each viewed the others as enemies in the past, they now consider each other as friends. Reyes speaks about what he has learned from being part of Boyle's program: "It's a lesson in that you don't have to kill your neighbors. It don't matter where you come from, what background you come from. We are all humans, and we should learn to live together."[69]

A Complex Issue

Tackling the issue of gangs is a tough challenge for law enforcement. Despite the various tactics that have been tried and programs that have been implemented, the number of gangs and gang members has continued to grow. In many communities, much of the violent crime is attributable to gangs. So what is the solution? Can gang violence be stopped? Those are questions that even the most seasoned criminal justice experts cannot answer with any certainty.

Can Gang Violence Be Stopped?

" Police gang units are often formed for the wrong reasons and perceived as isolated and ineffectual by law enforcement colleagues. "

—Judith Greene and Kevin Pranis, *Gang Wars: The Failure of Enforcement Tactics and the Need for Effective Safety Strategies,* Justice Policy Institute, July 2007. www.justicepolicy.org.

Greene and Pranis are criminal justice policy analysts.

....

" What wrong reasons would an agency form a gang unit for? Cities form gang units when there is an increase in gang-related crime. "

—Know Gangs, "Separating Fact from Fiction: The Truth Behind the Justice Policy Institute Report," July 1, 2007. www.knowgangs.com.

Know Gangs provides training to law enforcement personnel, educators, and social service workers to educate them about gangs, drugs, and school violence.

....

Bracketed quotes indicate conflicting positions.

* Editor's Note: While the definition of a primary source can be narrowly or broadly defined, for the purposes of Compact Research, a primary source consists of: 1) results of original research presented by an organization or researcher; 2) eyewitness accounts of events, personal experience, or work experience; 3) first-person editorials offering pundits' opinions; 4) government officials presenting political plans and/or policies; 5) representatives of organizations presenting testimony or policy.

66 No matter how formidable the challenges we face— no matter how forcefully gang violence threatens to tear our communities and our coalitions asunder—we must maintain our commitment to being neighbors, friends, partners, and allies. Standing together, we are more formidable than any adversary. And standing together, we will prevail. 99

—John S. Pistole, "2nd Los Angeles IACP Summit on Transnational Gangs, Los Angeles, California," *Major Executive Speeches*, Federal Bureau of Investigation, March 3, 2008. www.fbi.gov.

Pistole is deputy director of the Federal Bureau of Investigation.

66 To simply focus on enforcement without creating alternatives and support systems for the much larger numbers of kids on the periphery of gangs is the wrong direction. 99

—Steven D. Strachan, "Four Myths That Complicate Efforts to Confront Gang Violence," *Seattle Times*, January 29, 2009. http://seattletimes.nwsource.com.

Strachan is chief of police in Kent, Washington.

66 We cannot arrest our way out of our gang crime problem. We recognize that arrest is necessary to put hardened criminals away; however, we will fall far short of our overall goal if this is all that we do. 99

—William J. Bratton, "Exploring the National Criminal Justice Commission Act of 2009," testimony before the Senate Committee on the Judiciary Subcommittee on Crime and Drugs, June 11, 2009. www.lapdonline.org.

Bratton was chief of the Los Angeles Police Department from 2002 to 2009.

66 Law enforcement officers proactively fighting gangs, and crime in general, will see a valued success in the future leading for a safer tomorrow in the communities where gangs have previously flourished. 99

—Lou Savelli, "The Gang Terrorist Connection, Part II," *Corrections Connection*, June 2, 2008. www.corrections.com.

Savelli is a retired New York City police sergeant and cofounder of the East Coast Gang Investigators Association.

66 **The most important and effective provision of a gang injunction is the 'do not associate' requirement. A 'do not associate' provision restricts gang members' ability to gather in groups and consequently deters concerted actions.** 99

—Max Shiner, *Civil Gang Injunctions: A Guide for Prosecutors*, National District Attorneys Association, June 2009. www.ojp.usdoj.gov.

Shiner is the deputy district attorney for the city of Los Angeles.

....

66 **We oppose the anti-gang injunction provisions . . . because they raise serious constitutional concerns, create unintended consequences that will harm local communities and impede other anti-gang initiatives, and are based on a model that has had very limited effectiveness in reducing crime elsewhere.** 99

—Carl Takei, "Testimony on Behalf of the American Civil Liberties Union of the National Capital Area," testimony before the Committee on Public Safety and the Judiciary of the Council of the District of Columbia, May 18, 2009. www.aclu-nca.org.

Takei is a staff attorney with the American Civil Liberties Union (ACLU).

....

66 **Lengthy incarceration for the 'worst of the worst' can also have a deterrent effect on those contemplating gang life or those contemplating their criminal involvement in a gang.** 99

—Kathleen M. Rice, testimony, House Committee on Education and Labor, May 30, 2007. http://edlabor.house.gov.

Rice is the district attorney for Nassau County in Long Island, New York.

....

66 **While it is natural for us to ask how we can suppress and intervene in gang activity, focusing on this question may cause us to overlook the best strategy we have: prevention.** 99

—Gerald L. Zahorchak, testimony, Senate Judiciary Hearing, National Constitution Center, February 19, 2007. http://judiciary.senate.gov.

Zahorchak is Pennsylvania's secretary of education.

....

Facts and Illustrations

Can Gang Violence Be Stopped?

- Between 2001 and 2008, the FBI's Violent Gang Safe Street task force made nearly **41,000 arrests** leading to **16,666 convictions** for gang-related crime.

- Since implementation of an initiative known as Operation Community Shield in 2005, the Bureau of Immigration and Customs Enforcement (ICE) has arrested more than **8,000 gang members** from more than 700 gangs.

- FBI director John Pistole states that during 2007, joint gang investigations between his agency and city/state law enforcement led to over **2,300 convictions, 685 disruptions**, and **106 dismantlements** of gangs, and helped seize over **$27 million** in stolen property.

- According to former Los Angeles police chief William J. Bratton, because of law enforcement's crackdown on gangs, gang-related homicides in the city are down **26 percent** since 2008 and **63 percent** from 2002.

- Researchers have not been able to demonstrate that **gang injunctions** and other restrictions on association have the long-term effect of reducing crime.

- The FBI has more than **630 agents** dedicated to gang investigations and over **1,150 officers** who work on the Safe Streets violent gang initiative.

Gang Task Force Increases Arrests

Since 2001, the FBI has markedly increased its focus on the country's most violent gangs though programs such as Safe Streets Task Force initiative. This initiative consists of more than 2,000 local, state, and federal investigators that represent nearly 700 law enforcement agencies throughout the United States. This graph shows how gang member arrests, indictments, and convictions have steadily grown since the initiative has been in place.

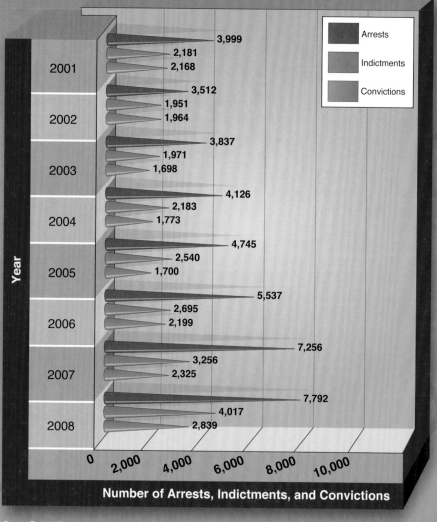

Legend: Arrests, Indictments, Convictions

2001: 3,999 / 2,181 / 2,168
2002: 3,512 / 1,951 / 1,964
2003: 3,837 / 1,971 / 1,698
2004: 4,126 / 2,183 / 1,773
2005: 4,745 / 2,540 / 1,700
2006: 5,537 / 2,695 / 2,199
2007: 7,256 / 3,256 / 2,325
2008: 7,792 / 4,017 / 2,839

Year

Number of Arrests, Indictments, and Convictions

0 2,000 4,000 6,000 8,000 10,000

Source: Federal Bureau of Investigation, "Fighting Gang Violence," July 2009. www.fbi.gov.

Targeting Illegal Immigrant Gangs

Hispanic gangs are the fastest-growing gang segment in the United States, and this is largely due to an influx of illegal immigrants, according to the Justice Department. From 2005 to 2007, as part of an initiative known as Operation Community Shield, officials from the Bureau of Immigration and, Customs Enforcement (ICE) arrested more than 8,000 gang members, more than three-fourths of whom were from Mexico and El Salvador. This chart shows the nationality breakdown of those who were arrested.

Operation Community Shield gang member arrests by nationality – 2005 to 2007

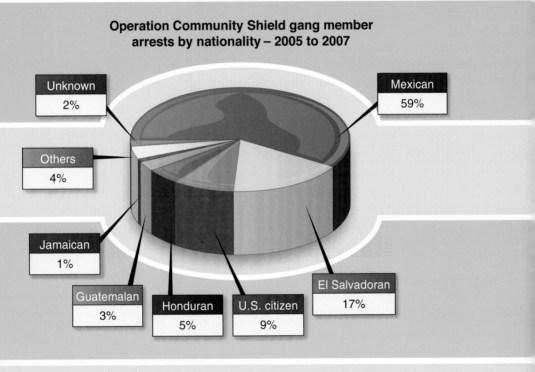

Unknown 2%

Mexican 59%

Others 4%

Jamaican 1%

Guatemalan 3%

Honduran 5%

U.S. citizen 9%

El Salvadoran 17%

Source: Jessica M. Vaughan and John D. Feere, "Taking Back the Streets: ICE and Local Law Enforcement Target Immigrant Gangs," Center for Immigration Studies *Backgrounder*, October 2008. www.cis.org.

- After Cincinnati, Ohio, implemented its Initiative to Reduce Violence in April 2007, the city saw a **38 percent** drop in gang-related homicides for the first six months in 2009.

- According to a July 2007 report by the Justice Policy Institute, spending on **gang law enforcement** has far outpaced spending on **gang prevention programs**.

75

Key People and Advocacy Groups

Alex Alonso: A nationally known historian and researcher who specializes in gangs and gang life.

Greg Boyle: A priest from Los Angeles who founded Homeboy Industries, a group that works with gang members by giving them jobs and helping them turn their lives around.

Gangs or Us: Founded by former Drug Enforcement Administration agent Robert Walker, Gangs or Us seeks to educate the public about gangs and gang-related activities.

Know Gangs: A leading training provider for law enforcement personnel, educators, and social service workers seeking to enhance their knowledge about gangs, drugs, and school violence.

Dashaun Morris: A former member of the Bloods who turned his life around after spending six months in prison and now counsels kids to help convince them to stay away from gangs.

National Gang Center: An organization that seeks to reduce gang involvement and levels of gang crime.

National Gang Intelligence Center: An agency of the U.S. Department of Justice that serves as a centralized intelligence resource for gang information and analytical support.

National Youth Violence Prevention Resource Center: Serves as a resource for communities that are working to prevent youth violence.

Lou Savelli: A retired New York City police sergeant who cofounded the East Coast Gang Investigators Association and its affiliate program, Gang Reduction Through Intervention, Prevention, and Education (GRIPE).

Street Gangs Resource Center: A group that seeks to help increase understanding of how and why the gang phenomenon has become so pervasive in society.

Robert Walker: A former agent with the U.S. Drug Enforcement Administration who now serves as a gang identification consultant.

Chronology

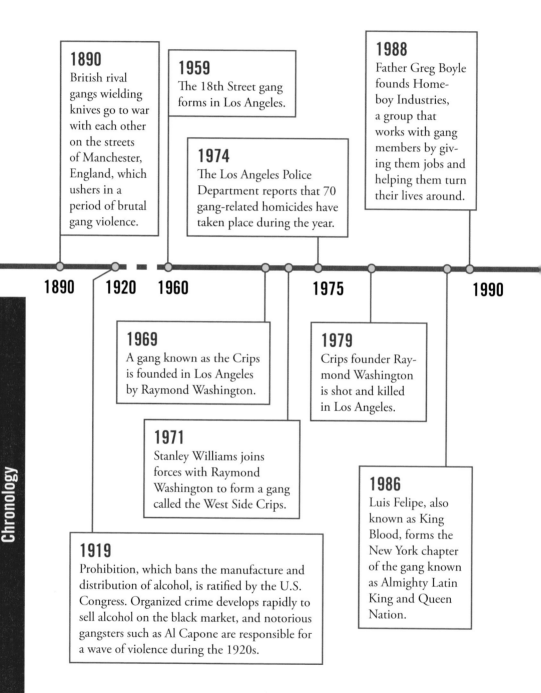

1890
British rival gangs wielding knives go to war with each other on the streets of Manchester, England, which ushers in a period of brutal gang violence.

1959
The 18th Street gang forms in Los Angeles.

1974
The Los Angeles Police Department reports that 70 gang-related homicides have taken place during the year.

1988
Father Greg Boyle founds Home-boy Industries, a group that works with gang members by giving them jobs and helping them turn their lives around.

1890   **1920**   **1960**   **1975**   **1990**

1969
A gang known as the Crips is founded in Los Angeles by Raymond Washington.

1979
Crips founder Raymond Washington is shot and killed in Los Angeles.

1971
Stanley Williams joins forces with Raymond Washington to form a gang called the West Side Crips.

1986
Luis Felipe, also known as King Blood, forms the New York chapter of the gang known as Almighty Latin King and Queen Nation.

1919
Prohibition, which bans the manufacture and distribution of alcohol, is ratified by the U.S. Congress. Organized crime develops rapidly to sell alcohol on the black market, and notorious gangsters such as Al Capone are responsible for a wave of violence during the 1920s.

1993
The United Blood Nation (the Bloods) gang forms within the New York City jail system on Rikers Island's George Mochen Detention Center.

2006
The National Center for Juvenile Justice releases a report entitled *Juvenile Offenders and Victims*, which estimates that 49 percent of gang members are Hispanic, 37 percent African American, 8 percent white, 5 percent Asian, and 1 percent of another ethnicity.

2004
The FBI forms the MS-13 National Gang Task Force to facilitate the exchange of information and intelligence among law enforcement agencies in order to combat the violent gang Mara Salvatrucha, better known as MS-13.

1990

2000

2010

1996
The United States passes legislation called the Illegal Immigration Reform and Immigrant Responsibility Act, which is aimed at reducing illegal immigration. It rapidly increases the pace of deportation of gang members.

2005
In its *National Gang Threat Assessment* report, the U.S. Department of Justice states that Asian gang activity is growing fastest in Chicago, New York City, and on the West Coast.

2008
The Federal Bureau of Investigation declares MS-13 to be America's most dangerous gang.

2009
A report by the National Gang Intelligence Center and National Drug Intelligence Center states that more than 20,000 gangs with a total of about 1 million members are criminally active in the United States.

Related Organizations

Center for Problem-Oriented Policing

1360 Regent St., PMB 323

Madison, WI 53715

phone: (704) 788-8302

e-mail: info@popcenter.org • Web site: www.popcenter.org

The Center for Problem-Oriented Policing seeks to provide information about ways that law enforcement can more effectively address specific crime issues. Its Web site links to a number of gang-related articles covering such topics as problem solving, at-risk youths, and the pros and cons of gang injunctions.

Federal Bureau of Investigation (FBI)

J. Edgar Hoover Building

935 Pennsylvania Ave. NW

Washington, DC 20535-0001

phone: (202) 324-3000

Web site: www.fbi.gov

The FBI's mission is to protect and defend the United States against terrorist and foreign intelligence threats and to enforce the country's criminal laws. Its Web site features news releases, statistics, speeches, and other publications related to gangs and gang violence.

Gang Reduction Through Intervention, Prevention, and Education (GRIPE)

c/o East Coast Gang Investigators Association

435 Alden Ave., Box #15

Morrisville, PA 19067

e-mail: ecgiamanagers@gmail.com • Web site: www.gripe4rkids.org

GRIPE seeks to raise awareness and educate communities about gangs and related problems. Its Web site features information about gang history, recruitment, myths, and school violence, as well as frequently asked questions about gangs and a forum where participants can discuss gang-related issues.

Gangs or Us

459 Oxenbridge Way

Chapin, SC 29036

phone: (803) 345-2600

e-mail: ganginfo@sc.rr.com • Web site: www.gangsorus.com

Gangs or Us was founded by Robert Walker, a former agent with the U.S. Drug Enforcement Administration who now serves as a gang identification consultant. The Web site offers a wealth of information about gangs and gang-related activities, including what defines a gang, the various types of gangs, frequently asked questions, and information for parents, teachers, and students.

Homeboy Industries

130 W. Bruno St.

Los Angeles, CA 90012

phone: (323) 526-1254 • fax: (323) 526-1257

e-mail: info@homeboy-industries.org

Web site: www.homeboy-industries.org

Founded in 1988 by Father Greg Boyle, Homeboy Industries works with gang members by giving them jobs and helping them turn their lives around. The Web site features a history section and information about Homeboy Industries programs and small businesses.

Justice Policy Institute

1012 14th St. NW, Suite 400

Washington, DC 20005

phone: (202) 558-7974

e-mail: info@justicepolicy.org • Web site: www.justicepolicy.org

The Justice Policy Institute seeks to promote effective solutions to society's problems that do not rely exclusively on incarceration. Its Web site links to the July 2007 report *Gang Wars: The Failure of Enforcement Tactics and the Need for Effective Public Safety Strategies*, as well as other publications.

Know Gangs

621 W. Racine St.

Jefferson, WI 53549

phone: (920) 674-4493

e-mail: director@ knowgangs.com • Web site: www.knowgangs.com

Founded by police officer Jared Lewis, Know Gangs is a leading training provider for law enforcement personnel, educators, and social service workers seeking to enhance their knowledge about gangs, drugs, and school violence. Its Web site links to news articles, videos, a newsletter, and an online forum.

National Gang Center

Institute for Intergovernmental Research

PO Box 12729

Tallahassee, FL 32317

phone: (850) 385-0600 • fax: (850) 386-5356

e-mail: information@nationalgangcenter.gov

Web site: www.nationalgangcenter.gov

The National Gang Center seeks to reduce gang involvement and levels of gang crime. Its Web site features an extensive section on frequently asked questions about gangs, as well as a list of resources, gang surveys, publications, and links to other informative sites.

National Gang Intelligence Center (NGIC)

Crystal City, VA

phone: (703) 414-8600 • fax: (703) 414-8554

Web site: www.justice.gov

The NGIC, which is an agency of the U.S. Department of Justice, serves as a centralized intelligence resource for gang information and analytical support. Its Web site's search engine produces numerous gang-related reports and statistics.

National Youth Violence Prevention Resource Center (NYVPRC)

PO Box 10809

Rockville, MD 20849

phone: (866) 723-3968 • fax: (301) 562-1001

Web site: www.safeyouth.org

The NYVPRC serves as a resource for communities that are working to prevent youth violence. Its Web site offers various publications on youth violence, as well as a search engine that produces numerous articles specifically related to gangs.

Street Gangs Resource Center

PO Box 18238

Los Angeles, CA 90018

phone: (800) 249-1324 • fax: (323) 686-5172

Web site: www.streetgangs.com

The Street Gangs Resource Center seeks to help increase understanding of how and why the gang phenomenon has become so pervasive in society. Its Web site offers a wealth of information about gangs including links to news articles, descriptions of the various types of gangs, research papers, video clips, and a bibliography.

U.S. Bureau of Justice Statistics

810 Seventh St. NW

Washington, DC 20531

phone: (202) 307-0765

e-mail: askbjs@usdoj.gov • Web site: www.ojp.gov

The Bureau of Justice Statistics is the primary source of criminal justice statistics compiled by the federal government. Its Web site links to numerous publications and news releases related to crime, the justice system, courts and sentencing, homicide trends, and the FBI's yearly Uniform Crime Reports.

Violence Prevention Institute

66 West Gilbert St., Suite 100

Red Bank, NJ 07701

phone: (973) 325-1958 • fax: (973) 323-2161

Web site: www.violencepreventioninstitute.org

The Violence Prevention Institute provides education, research, and prevention and intervention programs that address violent youth behavior. Its Web site offers publications, reports, news releases, and personal testimonials.

For Further Research

Books
William Dunn, *The Gangs of Los Angeles*. Lincoln, NE: iUniverse, 2007.

John M. Hagedorn, *A World of Gangs: Armed Young Men and Gangsta Culture*. Minneapolis: University of Minnesota Press, 2008.

Louis Kontos and David Brotherton, *Encyclopedia of Gangs*. Westport, CT: Greenwood, 2008.

Samuel Logan, *This Is for the Mara Salvatrucha: Inside the MS-13, America's Most Violent Gang*. New York: Hyperion, 2009.

Dashaun Morris, *War of the Bloods in My Veins: A Street Soldier's March Toward Redemption*. New York: Scribner, 2008.

William Queen, *Under and Alone: The True Story of the Undercover Agent Who Infiltrated America's Most Violent Outlaw Motorcycle Gang*. New York: Ballantine, 2007.

Tony Rafael, *The Mexican Mafia*. New York: Encounter, 2007.

Sudhir Venkatesh, *Gang Leader for a Day: A Rogue Sociologist Takes to the Streets*. New York: Penguin, 2008.

Periodicals
Veronika Belenkaya, "New Blood: Violent Gang Life Is Passed Down from Parent to Child," *New York Daily News*, June 15, 2008.

Rory Callinan, "Outbreak of Biker Violence Leaves Australia on Edge," *Time*, March 29, 2009.

Lisa A. Davis, "Out of the Gang," *Tampa Tribune*, May 20, 2007.

George Dohrmann, "How Dreams Die," *Sports Illustrated*, June 30, 2008.

Erik Eckholm, "Gang Violence Grows on an Indian Reservation," *New York Times*, December 14, 2009.

Sarah Garland, "Gangland in Suburbia," *New York Times*, June 21, 2009.

Madison Gray, "How to Turn Around a Gang Member," *Time*, September 2, 2009.

Jet, "Black Gangsters—or 'Any Black You See'—Were Targets of Latino Gangs in Los Angeles County, Investigation Reveals," January 21, 2008.

Alex Kingsbury, "The War on Gangs: Inside the Feds' Strategy to Get Hit Men and Enforcers off the Streets," *U.S. News & World Report*, December 15, 2008.

Kathleen Kingsbury, "Which Kids Join Gangs? A Genetic Explanation," *Time*, June 10, 2009.

Melissa Klein, "Gang Grief: Violence Wounds Teens and Communities," *Current Health 2*, March 2009.

Nancy Macdonald, "The Right Crowd: Gangster Murders Have Parents at Elite B.C. School Panicking," *Maclean's*, May 25, 2009.

Ken MacQueen, "How to Fight the Gangs: Gang-Related Crime Is Rising, Overwhelming the Authorities. But Something Can Be Done," *Maclean's*, March 16, 2009.

Mark Morris and Christine Vendel, "Why Do Kids Join Gangs? Ask the Students," *Kansas City Star*, December 2, 2007.

Lauren Todd Pappa, "Gangs: Keep Out! Three Teens Tell Why Gangs Are on the Rise and What You Can Do to Stay Safe," *Junior Scholastic*, November 26, 2007.

John Seabrook, "Don't Shoot," *New Yorker*, June 22, 2009.

Suzanne Smalley and Evan Thomas, "How Do You Leave a Gang?" *Newsweek*, February 16, 2009.

Boris Weintraub, "New Weapons in the Fight Against Gangs," *Parks & Recreation*, November 2009.

Internet Sources

Ted Braden, *Teen in Jail* blog. www.teeninjail.com.

Chris D'Amico, "A Survivor Sets Kids Straight on Myths of Gang Life," NJ Voices: Opinions from New Jersey blog, May 17, 2008. http://

blog.nj.com/njv_mark_diionno/2008/05/a_survivor_sets_kids_straight.html.

Federal Bureau of Investigation, "Gang Success Stories." www.fbi.gov/hq/cid/ngic/success.htm.

Ed Grabianowski, "How Street Gangs Work," How Stuff Works. http://people.howstuffworks.com/street-gang1.htm.

National Gang Intelligence Center and National Drug Intelligence Center, *National Gang Threat Assessment 2009*, January 2009. www.justice.gov/ndic/pubs32/32146/32146p.pdf.

Source Notes

Overview

1. Quoted in Cathleen Decker, "Melody Ross Touches the World," *Los Angeles Times*, November 8, 2009. www.latimes.com.
2. National Gang Intelligence Center and National Drug Intelligence Center, *National Gang Threat Assessment 2009*, January 2009. www.justice.gov.
3. Ed Grabianowski, "How Street Gangs Work," How Stuff Works. http://people.howstuffworks.com.
4. National Gang Intelligence Center and National Drug Intelligence Center, *National Gang Threat Assessment 2009*.
5. National Gang Intelligence Center and National Drug Intelligence Center, *National Gang Threat Assessment 2009*.
6. Quoted in Jason Trahan, "16 Dallas Killings May Be Prison Gang's Work," *Dallas Morning News*, February 15, 2007. www.knowgangs.com.
7. Quoted in Rosalio Ahumada, "Gang Infighting: When Members Attack Each Other, Bystanders Often Pay," *Modesto Bee*, June 15, 2009. www.modbee.com.
8. Judith Greene and Kevin Pranis, *Gang Wars: The Failure of Enforcement Tactics and the Need for Effective Safety Strategies*, Justice Policy Institute, July 2007. www.justicepolicy.org.
9. John S. Pistole, "2nd Los Angeles IACP Summit on Transnational Gangs, Los Angeles, California," Federal Bureau of Investigation *Major Executive Speeches*, March 3, 2008. www.fbi.gov.
10. ABC News, "Mean Streets: Gangs Going Digital," February 19, 2007. http://abclocal.go.com.
11. National Gang Intelligence Center and National Drug Intelligence Center, *National Gang Threat Assessment 2009*.
12. Quoted in Mark Morris and Christine Vendel, "Why Do Kids Join Gangs? Ask the Students," *Kansas City Star*, December 2, 2007. www.kansascity.com.
13. Quoted in Morris and Vendel, "Why Do Kids Join Gangs?"
14. Quoted in National Gang Intelligence Center and National Drug Intelligence Center, *National Gang Threat Assessment 2009*.
15. Quoted in Laura Angus, "'Gangs . . . Become Their Church': Girl Gangs Just as Deadly and Largely Ignored, Expert," *Flint Journal*, October 31, 2009. www.mlive.com.
16. Quoted in Greene and Pranis, *Gang Wars*.
17. Quoted in Chris D'Amico, "A Survivor Sets Kids Straight on Myths of Gang Life," NJ Voices: Opinions from New Jersey blog, May 17, 2008. http://blog.nj.com.
18. Pistole, "2nd Los Angeles IACP Summit on Transnational Gangs, Los Angeles, California."

How Serious a Problem Are Gangs?

19. Pistole, "2nd Los Angeles IACP Summit on Transnational Gangs, Los Angeles, California."
20. Center for Immigration Studies, "Taking Back the Streets: ICE and Local Law Enforcement Target Immigrant Gangs," *Backgrounder*, October 2008. www.cis.org.
21. Federal Bureau of Investigation, "A

Courageous Victim: Taking a Stand Against MS-13," May 1, 2009. www.fbi.gov.

22. Federal Bureau of Investigation, "A Courageous Victim."

23. Quoted in David Mattingly, "Minority Youngsters Dying Weekly on Chicago's Streets," CNN, May 8, 2009. www.cnn.com.

24. Quoted in Steve Patterson, Eric Herman, and Chris Fusco, "Chicago Gang Dispute Led to Killing on Bus," Police One, May 15, 2007. www.police one.com.

25. Quoted in Glenn Smith, "Incidence of Gang Violence Soaring," *Post and Courier* (Charleston, SC), December 10, 2009. www.postandcourier.com.

26. Gustav Eyler, "Gangs in the Military," *Yale Law Journal*, February 12, 2009. http://yalelawjournal.org.

27. National Gang Intelligence Center and National Drug Intelligence Center, *National Gang Threat Assessment 2009*.

28. Tony Rafael, *The Mexican Mafia*. New York: Encounter, 2007, p. 123.

29. Rafael, *The Mexican Mafia*, p. vii.

30. Rafael, *The Mexican Mafia*, p. viii.

31. Quoted in Damon Simms, "Youthful Gangs Have Mansfield Prison on Edge as Members Attack Other Convicts in Bands," Cleveland Live, April 11, 2009. http://blog.cleveland.com.

Why Do Young People Join Gangs?

32. Keith Ablow, interviewed by Jon Scott, "Gang Violence Growing in Suburban Areas Across the U.S.," FOX News, November 18, 2008. www.foxnews.com.

33. Dashaun Morris, *War of the Bloods in My Veins*. New York: Scribner, 2008, p. 23.

34. Morris, *War of the Bloods in My Veins*, p. 24.

35. Morris, *War of the Bloods in My Veins*, p. 13.

36. Morris, *War of the Bloods in My Veins*, p. 90.

37. Quoted in Peter Strescino, "Breaking the Gang Culture," *Pueblo* (CO) *Chieftain*, December 29, 2009. www.chieftain.com.

38. Anonymous, response to "Why Do You Think People Join Gangs? Have You Ever Been in a Gang?" Answer-Bag, December 9, 2007. www.answer bag.com.

39. Quoted in Veronika Belenkaya, "New Blood: Violent Gang Life Is Passed Down from Parent to Child," *New York Daily News*, June 15, 2008.

40. Quoted in Belenkaya, "New Blood."

41. Quoted in Belenkaya, "New Blood."

42. Quoted in Sofia Santana and Robert Nolin, "Suspects Called 'Trigger Happy,'" (South Florida) *Sun-Sentinel*, December 4, 2008. www.allbusiness.com.

43. Quoted in Kathleen Kingsbury, "Which Kids Join Gangs? A Genetic Explanation," *Time*, June 10, 2009. www.time.com.

Can People Leave the Gang Life Behind?

44. Quoted in Liz Carey, "Anderson Teens Share Gang Experiences, Difficulty of Getting Out," *Independent Mail*, October 26, 2009. www.independent mail.com.

45. Quoted in Carey, "Anderson Teens Share Gang Experiences, Difficulty of Getting Out."

46. Alex Alonso, "Departing from the Gang Can Be Easy," Street Gangs, August 23, 2009. www.streetgangs.com.

47. Alonso, "Departing from the Gang Can Be Easy."

48. Quoted in Jennifer Myers, "The Changing Face of Gang Culture in

Greater Lowell," *Lowell* (MA) *Sun*, December 8, 2009. www.lowellsun. com.

49. Quoted in Myers, "The Changing Face of Gang Culture in Greater Lowell."

50. Kellene Bishop, "Are You Prepared Against Organized Evil?" Preparedness Pro, 2009. www.preparednesspro. com.

51. Quoted in Greg Campbell, "Death by Deportation," *Fort Collins Now*, March 26, 2008. www.fortcollinsnow. com.

52. Robert Walker, "Background on Gang Initiations," Gangs or Us, September 25, 2009. www.gangsorus.com.

53. Michelle Arciaga, "Common Myths About Gangs," East Coast Gang Investigators Association, February 23, 2009. www.gripe4rkids.org.

54. Quoted in Kevin Johnson, "Families Relocate Gang Members to Save Them," *USA Today*, September 7, 2006. www.usatoday.com.

55. Quoted in Johnson, "Families Relocate Gang Members to Save Them."

56. Anonymous, response to "Why Do You Think People Join Gangs? Have You Ever Been in a Gang?" AnswerBag, December 9, 2007. www.answer bag.com.

Can Gang Violence Be Stopped?

57. Quoted in Alex Kingsbury, "The War on Gangs: Inside the Feds' Strategy to Get Hit Men and Enforcers off the Streets," *U.S. News & World Report*, December 15, 2008. www.usnews. com.

58. Know Gangs, "Separating Fact from Fiction: The Truth Behind the Justice Policy Institute Report," July 1, 2007.

www.knowgangs.com.

59. Quoted in John Seabrook, "Don't Shoot," *New Yorker*, June 22, 2009, p. 32+.

60. Quoted in Seabrook, "Don't Shoot."

61. Quoted in Seabrook, "Don't Shoot."

62. Quoted in Julie Bykowicz, "Juvenile Gangs," Crime Beat, *Baltimore Sun*, October 16, 2008. http://weblogs. baltimoresun.com.

63. Sudhir Venkatesh, in Stephan J. Dubner, "Everything You Always Wanted to Know About Street Gangs (but Didn't Know Whom to Ask)," Freakonomics, *New York Times*, August 6, 2007. http://freakonomics.blogs.nytimes. com.

64. Quoted in Paloma Esquivel, "Scores of O.C. Teens Picked Up in 'Scared Straight' Curfew Sweep," *Los Angeles Times*, November 13, 2009. http:// latimesblogs.latimes.com.

65. Los Angeles Police Department, "About Gang Injunctions." www.lapd online.org.

66. Venkatesh, in Dubner, "Everything You Always Wanted to Know About Street Gangs (but Didn't Know Whom to Ask)."

67. American Civil Liberties Union, "ACLU/SC Opposes Troubling Provisions of L.A. District Attorney's Proposed Gang Injunction in South Los Angeles," January 14, 2009. www. aclu-sc.org.

68. Quoted in Paul Harris, "Gang Mayhem Grips LA," *Guardian*, March 18, 2007. www.guardian.co.uk.

69. Quoted in Thelma Gutierrez and Wayne Drash, "Ex-Gang Members Unite: 'You Don't Have to Kill Your Neighbors,'" CNN, May 20, 2009. www.cnn.com.

List of Illustrations

Index

About the Author

Peggy J. Parks holds a bachelor of science degree from Aquinas College in Grand Rapids, Michigan, where she graduated magna cum laude. She has written more than 90 nonfiction educational books for children and young adults, as well as self-published a cookbook called *Welcome Home: Recipes, Memories, and Traditions from the Heart*. Parks lives in Muskegon, Michigan, a town that she says inspires her writing because of its location on the shores of Lake Michigan.